To Quit or Pivot

Navigating Buyer Agency in the Changing Landscape of Real Estate

Copyright © 2024 by Ericka L. Davis.

All rights reserved. November 2024

No part of this book may be reproduced, distributed, or transmitted in any form or by any means, including copying, electronic, or mechanical methods, without the author's prior written permission, except for brief quotations in reviews or other noncommercial uses as permitted by copyright law.

ISBN: 979-8-9919570-0-7 (eBook)

979-8-9919570-1-4 (Paperback)

Published by DavLone Publishing, a subsidiary of DavLone Holdings, LLC

Written by Ericka L. Davis

Cover Design by Layla L. Stewart

For permissions, inquiries, or further information, please contact:

www.realtybysignature.co Davlone Publishing Page

Disclaimer:

This book is for informational purposes only and does not constitute legal, financial, or professional advice. The author and publisher make no representations about the information's completeness or accuracy. Readers should consult with qualified professionals before making decisions based on this content.

The author and publisher disclaim any liability for any actions taken based on the information provided. The views expressed herein are those of the author and do not represent the views or policies of any organization, association, or agency referenced in this book. We hope this book is helpful for your journey and reminds you that professional advice is invaluable.

TABLE OF CONTENTS

INTRODUCTION 6

OPENING 9

CHAPTER 1
Understanding NAR: Industry Influence, Legal Challenges, the 2024 Settlement, and Why it Matters 15

CHAPTER 2
Re-wiring Real Estate: Redefining Transparency in the New Norm of Buyer Agency 37

CHAPTER 3
The P.I.E.R. Approach: Using Preparation, Innovation, Engagement & Retention to Attract and Retain Buyer Clients in This New Era of Real Estate 55

CHAPTER 4
Agency, Advocacy, and Advisory ... The Three 'A' Approach in Buyer Representation 85

CHAPTER 5
"To the Time Machine!" Buyer Agency in 2025 and Beyond, Preparing for the Future of Real Estate 95

CHAPTER 6
The Decision... to Quit or Pivot? Making Career Decisions in the Post-Settlement Landscape 109

USEFUL APPENDICES
    APPENDIX I. What Should I Say? 137
    APPENDIX II. What Is 'FOR SALE'? PART I. 144
    APPENDIX III. What is 'FOR SALE'? PART II. 149
    APPENDIX IV. Implementing the P.I.E.R Approach 155
    APPENDIX V. How to Talk *Compensation* 158
    APPENDIX VI. When to Talk *Compensation*. 161

REFERENCES 164

About the Author 168

INTRODUCTION

The real estate professional has entered a transformative era of agency. The industry's echoes are resonating loudly, with the internet abuzz and the traditional dynamics between buyer and seller agents evolving overnight. While consumers are being provided with step-by-step guidance, resources for real estate agents navigating this shift are still in their infancy. As real estate professionals, it seems as though we have been given guardrails but limited direction. This resource is designed to support real estate professionals assisting buyers as they navigate the challenges and opportunities in this changing landscape of real estate. In the following chapters, you will (1) gain insight, (2) equip yourself with tools, and (3) prepare to make informed decisions about the next steps in your career—whether in real estate or beyond.

This book serves as a detailed guide for real estate agents navigating the transformative changes introduced by the 2024 NAR Settlement. Prompted by lawsuits addressing alleged inflated commission structures, the settlement mandates significant shifts in transparency and collaboration between buyer & seller agents and, ultimately, the clients buyer & agents serve. These policy updates reshape how commissions are handled, requiring agents to adopt new approaches in compensation disclosure and client communication. Through this lens, this book explores the challenges and opportunities that lie ahead for buyer agents, helping them decide whether to remain in the industry or pivot to meet the demands of a more transparent, client-centered real estate environment.

At its core, this book introduces the P.I.E.R. Strategy—Preparation, Innovation, Engagement, and Retention—as a framework for agents who choose to adapt and thrive in this evolving landscape. It also emphasizes the Three 'A' Approach—Agency, Advocacy, and Advisory—encouraging agents to enhance client relationships by focusing on trust and expertise. Additionally, the chapters cover the future of buyer agency and the tools needed for success, including specialized skills, niche service models, and client-centered practices. By combining practical strategies with thoughtful reflection exercises, this book empowers agents to make informed, confident career decisions that align with both their professional strengths and personal goals in a changing real estate industry.

OPENING

In this buyer agency scenario, have you been wondering what to do?

A market scenario as of—August 17, 2024. A hopeful homebuyer contacts you, expressing interest in viewing available properties. As a Buyer's Agent, what is your next move? If you have recently found yourself saying:

> "I don't know what to do, so I'm just not calling the Hopeful Homebuyer back."
>
> "Hopeful Homebuyer, I'll get right back to you"— but then never follow up.
>
> "Hopeful Homebuyer, just sign this agreement!"— with little clarity on what comes next.
>
> "Hopeful Homebuyer, I'm referring you to a Buyer's Agent because I no longer represent buyers."

Or even,

ERICKA L. DAVIS

> *"Hopeful Homebuyer, I'm referring you to someone else because I'm quitting real estate altogether."*

Agents have faced this scenario daily since August 17, 2024. This resource provides insightful approaches to face and perform successfully in your response.

Background

The National Association of Realtors ("NAR") is the largest trade association for real estate professionals in the United States. Founded in 1908, NAR advocates for real estate agents, brokers, and industry policies on a national scale, offering members resources, industry data, and professional development opportunities. According to LeadsDeposit.com, as of early 2024, the U.S. had approximately three million licensed real estate agents. NAR statistics indicate that half (1.5 million) of these agents are members of NAR. Regardless of membership, NAR's decisions and leadership impact the day-to-day practices of **all** real estate professionals nationwide. The 2024 NAR Settlement exemplifies this influence, introducing significant changes to real estate practices across the industry.

In early 2024, NAR entered into a preliminary settlement agreement in response to multiple lawsuits filed by home sellers. These lawsuits alleged that NAR's practices and those of several co-defendant real estate companies contributed to inflated commission structures. As part of this settlement, NAR agreed to implement significant policy and practice updates to reshape collaboration between seller and buyer agents. These changes are designed to reform commission practices and bring greater transparency to real estate transactions industry-wide.

Effective August 17, 2024, these comprehensive updates mark a new era for real estate professionals. This book will unpack the details of the NAR settlement, its implications for agents that support buyers, and the pivotal decision facing buyer agents: whether to exit the industry or pivot to thrive in a transforming market.

This book is not about quitting; it is about pivoting. Making the right adjustments now will allow you to not just survive but thrive in this emerging reality of real estate in the United States. You have the foundation, and now it is time to build on it. The world of real estate is evolving, and buyer agents everywhere are grappling with the implications of the recent NAR settlement and their ability to evolve with the industry. Understandably, many may feel uncertain about what this means for their careers and clients. However, as the saying goes, with change comes opportunity, and this book is about readying yourself to seize that opportunity. Here is what you can expect from the upcoming chapters:

- **Plain English Answers.** You will find clear, straightforward explanations to guide you through the complexities of the settlement and what it means for your role as a buyer agent. We will break down the jargon and legal language, helping you understand the premise for the core shifts in the market.

- **A Framework for Growth.** In a realty world that is shifting, those who pivot and adjust will be the ones who move forward. Together, we will explore strategies that will help you continue to grow your realty business in 2024 and beyond. Whether it is refining your marketing, embracing new technology, or rethinking the buyer-agent relationship, these chapters will provide actionable steps to keep you competitive.

- **A Time for Opportunity.** Change is never easy, but it can also be a catalyst for growth. Now is the time to engage your growth mindset. Instead of fearing the unknown, this resource will help you see the immense potential that lies in the evolving real estate market. With the right mindset and tools, you can position yourself not just as an agent who survives this transformation, but as one who leads the charge into the future.

This book provides agents with actionable guidance and insights to successfully navigate the post-settlement landscape. Whether an agent chooses to stay, pivot, or transition into a new role, agents are encouraged to embrace adaptability, transparency, and a commitment to client satisfaction as the foundation of long-term success in the real estate field.

As the real estate industry continues to evolve, agents must understand the forces shaping the landscape they operate within. The 2024 NAR settlement marks a significant turning point that requires agents to stay informed and adaptable. To effectively navigate this new environment, it is essential to examine the role of the National Association of Realtors ("NAR"), the legal challenges it has faced, and the far-reaching implications of the settlement. **Chapter 1. Understanding NAR: Influence, Legal Challenges, the 2024 Settlement, and Why it Matters ...** will explore these essential elements, providing a deeper understanding of how they impact the future of real estate and why these changes matter to every agent moving forward.

CHAPTER 1

Understanding NAR: Industry Influence, Legal Challenges, the 2024 Settlement, and Why it Matters

Industry Influence

The National Association of Realtors ("NAR") is the largest trade association in the United States, representing over 1.5 million real estate professionals, including agents, brokers, and other real estate specialists. It is a prominent organization that significantly influences the practices and the pulse of the real estate industry. NAR advocates for real estate professionals and shapes policy and legislation affecting the real estate market. Some of these influencing roles include:

- setting professional and practice standards for its membership,
- providing resources and education, and
- advocating for policies that support its members' interests at municipal, state, and federal levels.

Additionally, NAR provides standards that influence the operation of Multiple Listing Services ("MLS"). MLSs are databases created, maintained, and paid for by real estate professionals to help facilitate the buying and selling of properties. The National Association of Realtors and Multiple

Listing Services are closely connected, as NAR has been instrumental in developing, maintaining, and regulating many MLSs across the United States. Here is how NAR and MLSs are related and how they impact real estate:

- **NAR's Role in MLS Development.** Historically, NAR played a significant role in creating and promoting MLSs to foster cooperation among real estate professionals. By standardizing property listings and enabling agents to share information, NAR helped MLSs become essential tools for real estate transactions.

- **MLS Oversight by Local Member Associations.** While NAR does not directly operate MLSs, many are managed by local and regional member associations affiliated with NAR. These associations set the rules, regulations, and membership criteria for MLS access, often aligning with NAR's policies and code of ethics. This connection ensures that many MLSs follow ethical standards and professional practices consistent with NAR's guidelines.

- **Membership and MLS Access.** Most MLSs require that agents and brokers are NAR members to gain access. This membership structure means that agents who want full MLS access must typically be members of NAR, adhering to its code of ethics and paying membership fees. However, some MLSs offer access to non-members, though usually with restrictions and additional fees.

- **Impact on Property Information Access.** NAR and MLSs work together to create a centralized, organized system for property information. Through MLSs, its members have exclusive access to extensive property details, pricing history, and other data, which they can use to serve clients effectively. MLS databases also enable its members to market properties widely, attracting more buyers and providing greater exposure for listings.

- **Policy Influence and Industry Standards.** NAR's influence on MLSs extends to policy-making and industry standards. Through its legal and regulatory efforts, NAR establishes guidelines that impact MLS rules, including policies on data sharing, listing practices, and agent cooperation.

- **Public Access to MLS Listings.** While full MLS access is typically limited to its members, many MLSs offer public access through listing websites (like Realtor.com, which NAR owns) to give consumers general property information. However, only licensed members with full MLS access can view complete property data and provide clients with in-depth insights.

The National Association of Realtors and Multiple Listing Services work closely to support the real estate industry. NAR's standards, ethics, and policies shape MLS practices, creating a collaborative environment for agents and providing essential visibility for property listings. This influence extends across the industry through NAR's guidelines, professional code of ethics, and lobbying efforts. Under NAR's MLS guidelines, it became standard practice for listing brokers to offer commissions to buyer brokers—a tradition that has shaped commission structures throughout the industry.

Beyond MLS practices, NAR exercises significant lobbying power, consistently working to influence housing policies at local, state, and national levels. Through lobbying efforts, NAR advocates for laws and regulations supporting real estate professionals, property owners, and the housing market. Key elements of NAR's advocacy include initiatives aimed at preserving the interests of its members while fostering a stable, equitable real estate landscape. Key aspects of NAR's lobbying efforts are:

- **Influence in Federal Legislation.** NAR plays an active role in shaping federal housing policies through direct lobbying and political contributions. For instance, the organization has lobbied for tax policies that benefit homeowners, such as the mortgage interest deduction, and it has opposed legislative changes that could negatively affect homeownership, like proposed limits on the deduction in tax reform discussions.

- **Political Action Committees ("PACs").** NAR operates an influential political action committee, the Realtors Political Action Committee ("RPAC"), which contributes funds to support political candidates who advocate for real estate-friendly policies. RPAC is among the top contributors in federal elections, and its financial influence extends to state and local races as well.

- **Local and state advocacy.** NAR also supports local and state associations in their advocacy for housing policies. These efforts include working on issues such as zoning laws, property taxes, and affordable housing. By engaging with legislators at all levels, NAR helps craft policies that impact local housing markets and real estate transactions.

- **Advocacy for Property Rights.** A core part of NAR's lobbying agenda is the protection of property rights. The organization frequently pushes for legislation that safeguards the rights of property owners, fights against policies that could impose unnecessary burdens on property transactions and supports affordable housing initiatives that encourage homeownership.

NAR has successfully lobbied for various policies, such as:
- The preservation of 1031 like-kind exchanges, which allow real estate investors to defer capital gains taxes when they reinvest in new properties.
- Pandemic-era relief efforts, where NAR advocated for real estate professionals to be included in stimulus packages and received support for rental assistance programs.

You may ask...Why are NAR's influence and roles a critical catalyst to the changing landscape of real estate? These efforts highlight what is viewed as NAR's substantial role in shaping housing policy to benefit its members and the broader real estate market. Unfortunately, this role may have also had a foundational impact on the legal challenges of the past and the legal challenges that it faces in the present.

Legal Challenges of the Past and Present: The Catalysts to the 2024 NAR Settlement

United States v. National Association of Real Estate Boards. (1950) was the first major lawsuit involving antitrust concerns against NAR, via its predecessor, the National Association of Real Estate Boards ("NAREB"). The U.S. Department of Justice ("DOJ") sued the National Association of Real Estate Boards in a complaint that focused on NAREB's practice of setting mandatory commission rates. The DOJ argued that this practice constituted illegal price fixing and violated antitrust laws. The key elements of United States v. National Association of Real Estate Boards (1950) were:

- **Antitrust Violations.** The case centered on alleged antitrust violations, with the government arguing that the National Association of Real Estate Boards engaged in practices that restricted competition and set fixed commission rates.

- **Price-Fixing.** The court examined whether NAREB's practices constituted price-fixing by setting standard commission rates among real estate agents, which could limit consumer choice and inflated prices.

- **Impact on Interstate Commerce.** A significant aspect of the case was whether NAREB's actions affected interstate commerce, making them subject to federal antitrust laws.

The Supreme Court ultimately ruled that NAREB's actions did violate the Sherman Antitrust Act by restricting competitive practices, setting a precedent that industry associations cannot engage in activities that restrict competition. This decision underscored the legal boundaries within which real estate associations must operate, influencing how real estate boards set policies around commissions and cooperation among agents.

ERICKA L. DAVIS

The outcome. The U.S. Department of Justice won the case, and the ruling forced NAREB to cease enforcing mandatory commission rates. This decision set a legal precedent, establishing that real estate boards could not dictate commission structures, paving the way for more competition within the industry. This case laid foundational guidelines for antitrust compliance in the real estate industry, with enduring relevance for practices around commission structures and agent cooperation for the future.

The U.S. DOJ v. NAREB (1950) case holds significant importance as it was one of the first cases to challenge the practices of real estate boards, leading to substantial changes in the handling of commissions in real estate transactions. Consequently, this case seems to have laid the groundwork for subsequent antitrust scrutiny of NAR's past and present practices and policies. This case may have also created a foundation for NAR's legal disputes of the present. We will explore the 2019 lawsuits that ultimately led to the 2024 NAR Settlement Agreement.

- **Scott and Rhonda Burnett et al. v. National Association of Realtors, et al., Case No. 19-CV-332-SRB, U.S. District**

Court for the Western District of Missouri (2019) (commonly known as the "Sitzer/Burnett Lawsuit"). The Sitzer-Burnett lawsuit is a class action lawsuit brought by home sellers in Missouri, who alleged that the National Association of Realtors and several large real estate firms conspired to maintain artificially high commission rates through restrictive commission-sharing policies on the platforms known as the Multiple Listing Service.

- **Christopher Moehrl et al. v. National Association of Realtors, et al., Case No. 1:19-cv-01610, filed in the U.S. District Court for the Northern District of Illinois on March 19, 2019 (commonly known as the "Moehrl Lawsuit").** This case is a class action lawsuit brought by home sellers, led by plaintiff Christopher Moehrl, against the National Association of Realtors. It also included several major real estate companies as co-defendants. The plaintiffs allege that the defendants engaged in antitrust practices related to real estate commissions and MLS policies; they claim these practices led to artificially high commission rates.

ERICKA L. DAVIS

Why were the National Association of Realtors and other real estate companies sued in 2019?

So, you ask, *"Why were the National Association of Realtors and other real estate companies sued in 2019?"* The National Association of Realtors (and co-defendants) were sued for purportedly conspiring to use a "mandatory" Buyer Broker Commission Rule as a means to require home sellers to pay the fees of the broker representing the buyer of their homes and to pay these fees at an inflated amount, *in violation of federal antitrust law*. According to the plaintiff's complaint (paraphrasing here), the alleged conspiracy has imposed costs on home sellers that the buyer would otherwise cover in a *competitive market* if not for NAR's established practices. Plaintiffs further claim that this conspiracy has driven up buyer broker commissions, consequently inflating the overall commission costs borne by home sellers, who, on average, have incurred thousands of dollars in damages due to these alleged practices. **Does this sound familiar?**

The *United States DOJ v. National Association of Real Estate Boards* (1950) was considered precedent in the Sitzer/Burnett case, as both the 1950 complaint and the 2019 Sitzer/Burnett complaint involve allegations of anti-competitive practices by NAR related to setting mandatory commission rates. The 1950 DOJ v. NAREB case established that such practices violate antitrust laws. Thus providing a legal foundation for the arguments made in the Sitzer/Burnett lawsuit. Drawing on the 1950 precedent, the Sitzer/Burnett legal team achieved a landmark jury verdict in October 2023 that sent shockwaves through the real estate industry. The jury awarded $1.785 billion to the plaintiffs in the Sitzer/Burnett case.

The Sitzer/Burnett verdict is viewed as a historic ruling in real estate anti-trust litigation, setting a precedent for future industry practices. With other pending litigation sharing the same core claims as the DOJ and Sitzer/Burnett cases, NAR chose not to pursue an appeal and instead moved forward with a settlement.

The 2024 NAR Settlement Agreement

Now often referred to as the "NAR Settlement," this resolution addresses a series of individual and class action lawsuits filed by home sellers against NAR and several prominent real estate firms. On March 15, 2024, this series of individual and class action lawsuits with similar claims were consolidated for the purpose of settlement. The National Association of Realtors and home sellers received preliminary approval of the settlement terms from the Court on April 23, 2024. The final approval hearing is set for November 26, 2024. The settlement agreement settles the legal matters of:

- *Sitzer – Burnett, et al. v. The National Association of Realtors, et al.*, No. 19-cv-00332-SRB, U.S. District Court Western District of Missouri, Western Division (2019).

- *Moehrl, et al. v. The National Association of Realtors, et al.*, No. 1:19-cv-01610-ARW, In the U.S. District Court Northern District of Illinois, Eastern Division (2019).

KEY terms of the NAR Settlement

1. A Grant of Dismissal with Prejudice & Release of Liability of NAR and approximately two-thirds of its membership, including:
   - Over one million NAR members
   - All state/territorial and local REALTOR® associations.
   - All association-owned MLSs

- All brokerages with a NAR member as the principal party, if their residential transaction volume in 2022 did not exceed $2 billion that met certain criteria.

2. Industry-wide injunctive relief, which requires fundamental changes in its practices. These mandated changes include:
    - Eliminating the requirement for listing brokers to offer commissions to buyer agents on the MLS.
    - Requiring buyer agents to enter written agreements with clients that clarify the agent's compensation.
    - Enhancing transparency around commission rates and promoting competitive practices within real estate transactions.

3. A settlement payment of $418 million to be paid by NAR over approximately a four (4) year period; and lastly

4. NAR maintains its position that cooperative compensation is in the best interest of consumers and continues to deny any wrongdoing.

ERICKA L. DAVIS

Now that we have a brief overview of NAR, its impact, and its legal challenges...

Why does (*or should*) the 2024 NAR Settlement Matter to the Buyer Agent?

The 2024 NAR Settlement marks a transformative shift in modern real estate practice, especially in how buyer agents and seller agents collaborate. Previously, agent compensation was typically set by the seller and was not part of the purchase negotiation, allowing the transaction to focus solely on the property sale without the influence of agent fees. However, under the settlement's new guidelines, agent compensation must now be discussed openly, bringing it into the negotiation process and prompting significant adjustments in how agents engage with clients and collaborate. This change brings about a new level of transparency. Furthermore, agents must adjust to a dual negotiation model and reorganize the real estate services offered in each transaction.

Let us further explore the primary requirements of the settlement and examine why understanding the 2024 NAR Settlement is essential to the progression of buyer agency:

- **Unlinking of Commissions.** Traditionally, the commissions for both buyer and seller agents were bundled into a single transaction cost, paid by the seller. The settlement encourages a shift toward separating these fees, enabling more open negotiation of buyer agent compensation. Previously, buyer agents' commissions were paid from the seller's proceeds, with the manner of distribution of cooperative commissions often set by MLS rules and managed by the listing agent. Now, with greater transparency and the option for buyer agents to negotiate fees directly with clients and vice versa, agents may need to adapt to a model where they secure their compensation rather than relying on seller-paid commissions.

- **Transparency of Commissions.** A central issue in the lawsuit was the lack of clarity around buyer agent compensation. The settlement now requires real estate agents to disclose their exact commission, allowing buyers to see clearly what portion goes to their agent. This transparency may prompt buyers to question commission amounts or negotiate for lower fees, which could, in turn, impact the earnings of buyer agents.

- **Increased Negotiability and Evolving Client Expectations.** With the introduction of transparent fee structures, buyer agents may need to deliver more value-added services to justify their commissions. This shift encourages agents to reconsider and potentially enhance the service packages they offer as buyers become increasingly aware of the costs involved in their representation. Buyers now have greater freedom to negotiate their agent's compensation (formerly referred to as "commission") rather than having it automatically bundled into the transaction, making it essential for agents to clearly communicate the unique value they bring to the table.

- **Potential for greater competition.** The settlement may encourage alternative commission models and new competitors, such as discount brokerages or a la carte services, where buyers pay only for specific services they need. Buyer agents may need to effectively differentiate themselves to stay competitive in this shifting landscape. As buyers become more informed about fees and services, agents will feel increased pressure to clearly communicate and justify their unique value proposition to clients.

The NAR Settlement has ushered in an emerging era of transparency within the real estate industry. Following landmark lawsuits and a significant settlement, NAR agreed to implement changes that address long-standing consumer concerns surrounding commission structures and agent compensation. Previously, commission-sharing practices on the MLS often lacked transparency, leaving home sellers unclear on how fees were set or whether they could be negotiated.

While these changes present new challenges, they also offer opportunities for agents willing to pivot and embrace updated compensation models and client-centered practices. Buyer agents who can effectively communicate their value, deliver outstanding service, and prioritize transparency are likely to succeed in this new landscape. Those who innovate by offering flexible service models or cost-effective solutions may find growth opportunities in an increasingly competitive market. Understanding the 2024 NAR Settlement and its implications is essential for agents to thrive in this evolving environment.

As the real estate landscape shifts, agents who are ready to adapt can position themselves at the forefront of this transitioning era. Embracing updated compensation models and a client-centered approach is not just about compliance—it is a chance to redefine the standard for buyer agency.

Reader Reflect and Review

Identify Key Points. List three significant ways the NAR has influenced real estate industry practices. How do these influences impact your role as an agent today?

(1) _____

_____

_____

(2) _____

_____

_____

(3) _____

_____

Legal Impacts. Reflect on the 2024 NAR Settlement. What do you think is the most important change resulting from the settlement? How might it affect your approach to buyer agency?

Action Step. Based on what you've learned, what is one thing you can do to align your practices with the new industry standards introduced by the NAR Settlement?

_____

_____

_____

_____

_____

_____

In the next chapter, **Re-wiring Real Estate: Redefining Transparency in the New Norm of Buyer Agency**, we will explore how transparency is reshaping client relationships, the agent's role, and the overall structure of buyer representation. Understanding these changes will empower agents to not only meet new expectations but also to build trust and credibility in an increasingly open, client-focused market.

CHAPTER 2

Re-wiring Real Estate: Redefining Transparency in the New Norm of Buyer Agency

ERICKA L. DAVIS

Redefining Transparency

Post-settlement, NAR's updated policies ensure that buyers actively select and compensate the buyer's agent. The settlement introduces substantial changes in how buyer agents operate, particularly emphasizing transparency and clarity. These changes aim to increase consumer awareness, promote informed decision-making, and enhance competition within the real estate industry.

Transparency is the practice of openly sharing information in a clear, accessible, and straightforward manner. In business and professional settings, transparency involves being honest and upfront about costs, processes, and decision-making so that all parties have a shared understanding. This approach builds trust, enabling others to see and understand the motivations, methods, and actions behind decisions or practices being performed on their behalf. Transparency transforms buyer agency and redefines how agents engage with clients in the post-settlement real estate market. This chapter delves into how transparency is highlighted as a cornerstone in buyer agency, reshaping traditional practices and expectations.

This shift requires agents to adopt new communication, compensation, and client service approaches. To effectively convey your role as a buyer representative and fully understand your client's expectations, the delivery of buyer agency should focus on the following key areas.

Building Trust Through Open Communication. To build trust and clarity from the start, introduce your services and associated fees early in the relationship. This proactive approach shows clients that you prioritize openness and lays a foundation for trust. The way buyer agents are compensated has evolved. While real estate professionals are aware of this change, many homebuyers may not be. Today's reality is that prospective homebuyers' financial obligations can increase when they choose to work with a buyer's agent. Clear, confident communication with buyers sets the tone for productive discussions around fees and services.

Lead with clarity! Real estate transactions are complex, and agent compensation can be easily misunderstood in today's environment. Use simple, non-technical language to explain your compensation structure, outline what is included, and clarify what may be negotiable. This straightforward approach helps clients understand your value without being overwhelmed by industry jargon. When discussing compensation, focus on addressing costs, answering client questions, and positioning transparency as a core part of your relationship. This approach builds trust and empowers clients to make informed decisions.

Transparent Disclosure of Agency Compensation. Real estate agency is primarily governed by state law, with each state establishing its own laws, regulations, and licensing requirements. These cover various aspects of real estate practice, including agency relationships, fiduciary duties, and licensing standards. However, federal laws also impact real estate practices, particularly in areas such as fair housing, anti-discrimination, and antitrust compliance. National laws, like the Fair Housing Act and the Sherman Antitrust Act, prohibit discrimination and anti-competitive practices across the industry. Because of state-specific regulations, buyer representation agreements may vary from state to state. Yet, all agreements for buyer representation between a buyer's agent and a prospective homebuyer must clearly disclose the compensation arrangement between the agent's brokerage and the buyer.

Notably, the enforceable agreement is between the **agent's brokerage and the buyer.** This detail is important because the compensation structure presented to the buyer is primarily determined or authorized by the brokerage's policies to which the agent affiliates. Although the brokerage sets the overall framework of the compensation structure, there is room for negotiation [between the agent and the buyer] on payment terms. For example, suppose the brokerage offers a tiered compensation program, but the buyer prefers a flat-fee program. In that case, the agent may not have the authority to alter the brokerage's established compensation programs. It is crucial for both agents and clients to have a clear understanding of the brokerage's compensation options upfront and how the roles of the brokerage and agent align in the buyer's home purchase process.

To accommodate buyers with varying budgets and purchasing power, many brokerages are innovating with flexible fee structures that offer a range of service levels at different price points. This approach allows buyers to choose the compensation structure that best suits their needs, giving buyer agents the ability to work within their clients' financial comfort levels. Adopting a flexible approach to compensation not only enables buyers to find a service level that fits their budget but also enhances transparency overall in real estate transactions. With varying fee structures now available, the need for clear, upfront communication about agency compensation is more essential than ever.

In this new landscape, buyer agents are compensated in a way that aligns more closely with the value they bring to the table, making the process more transparent and client-centered. As a buyer agent, this structure enables you to define your worth clearly, while clients gain the freedom to choose the services and compensation structures that best meet their needs.

As brokerages adapt their compensation structures and prioritize open communication, buyer expectations are evolving in response to this emerging era of transparency. Understanding and meeting these shifting expectations is key for buyer agents aiming to build trust and deliver value. This brings us to our next topic, *Navigating Evolving Buyer Expectations in a Transparent Market.*

Navigating Evolving Buyer Expectations in a Transparent Market. Transparency significantly impacts buyer expectations, particularly regarding service quality, value, and ethical practices. In a transparent market, buyers are more informed and expect higher professionalism and honesty from the agents they retain. Service quality, value, and ethical practices are key qualities shaping these heightened expectations.

When an agent clearly communicates their role, fees, and services, buyers understand what to expect. Transparency in service offerings raises buyer expectations for consistent, high-quality service, as buyers can see exactly what they are paying for. They expect agents to follow through on commitments and deliver exceptional service, with each aspect of the transaction openly disclosed. Given buyers' increased awareness of commission structures, ensuring that the services you offer are well-defined and understood is essential. Buyers are now paying closer attention to the scope and quality of services, so these must be comprehensive and clearly communicated.

With transparent fee structures, buyers are more aware of the direct costs associated with representation and, as a result, look for clear value in return. They expect agents to justify their fees through demonstrated expertise, market knowledge, and a commitment to client success. To manage service expectations in today's real estate market, agents should clearly outline the full range of services included in the buyer representation agreement. As a buyer's agent, highlight your role in the property search, market analysis, negotiation process, and transaction management. Additionally, be knowledgeable about your authority to customize service offerings based on the client's priorities—especially if the client is focused on saving money or negotiating a lower fee. Transparency makes buyers more selective, as they now seek tangible benefits, such as effective negotiation skills, insightful advice, and efficient transaction management, which align with their financial investment.

Transparency also fosters trust, raising buyer expectations around ethical conduct. Buyers now anticipate honest communication, accurate information, and full disclosure of any potential conflicts of interest. Transparent practices reinforce the agent's role as a trusted advisor, and buyers expect agents to act in their best interests, prioritizing integrity and fairness throughout the transaction. By promoting transparency, agents meet these elevated expectations and strengthen their client relationships, enhancing their reputation as ethical and reliable professionals in a more client-centered market.

In a transparency-driven market, buyer's agents must be prepared to navigate with confidence, prioritizing clear communication, adaptable service options, and a strong value proposition to build and maintain trust. By embracing open communication and a client-centered approach, agents can stay relevant and responsive to the evolving expectations of today's buyers. Equipped with these essential tools, agents are well-positioned to thrive and succeed in a market where transparency is the foundation of lasting client relationships.

1. **Managing Buyer Expectations and the Overall Service Experience.** Effectively managing buyer expectations is crucial for delivering a high-quality service experience. Buyers are becoming more informed than ever, with clear expectations around transparency, personalized service, and open communication. For buyer agents, setting the tone early and maintaining a responsive approach throughout the transaction can make all the difference in client satisfaction and long-term loyalty. Here are key

strategies for managing expectations and enhancing the overall service experience.

2. **Setting Clear Expectations from the Start.** The foundation of a positive service experience is established from the very first interaction. During initial consultations, agents should outline the buying process, explain their role, and clarify what clients can expect at each stage. This includes discussing (a) the scope of services, (b) agent availability, (c) transaction timelines, (d) potential challenges, and, importantly, (e) service fees and/or compensation. By being transparent about these elements upfront, agents foster trust and reduce the likelihood of misunderstandings later.

Clear expectations also involve helping buyers understand the current market dynamics. Whether the market is competitive or slower-paced, agents can explain how these conditions may impact property searches, offers, and negotiations. When clients have a realistic picture of what is ahead, they are better prepared to navigate the process with confidence.

3. **Communicating Regularly and Proactively.** Ongoing communication is key to managing buyer expectations and ensuring a smooth transaction experience. Proactive updates on new listings, changes in market conditions, and transaction milestones keep buyers informed and engaged. Rather than waiting for clients to ask questions, agents can anticipate needs and provide updates before clients even think to ask.

   This consistent communication not only reassures buyers but also demonstrates the agent's commitment to their success. For example, suppose a buyer is facing a competitive market. In this case, regular updates and reminders about what to expect during the offer process can help alleviate stress and maintain a sense of control.

4. **Personalizing the Service Experience.** Personalization is another essential element of managing expectations and enhancing service. By understanding each buyer's unique needs, goals, and concerns, agents can tailor their approach and provide a more customized experience. This might involve sending listings that match a buyer's specific criteria, providing neighborhood insights, or offering targeted advice based on the buyer's priorities.

When clients see that their agent is responsive to their individual needs, they feel valued and understood. Personalization not only helps set realistic expectations but also strengthens the client-agent relationship, as clients recognize that their agent is genuinely invested in helping them achieve their goals.

5. **Educating Clients on the Value of Buyer Representation.** In a transparency-driven market, buyers are often aware of the costs associated with representation and may have questions about the value they are receiving. To manage these expectations, agents should clearly articulate the benefits of buyer representation, from market expertise to negotiation skills. Agents can explain how their services go beyond simply finding properties, emphasizing their role in securing favorable terms, handling complex paperwork, and guiding clients through the entire transaction.

By helping clients understand the full scope of services, buyer's agents can justify their fees and reinforce the value they bring to the table. This approach not only sets realistic expectations but also enhances the buyer's appreciation of the agent's expertise and dedication.

6. **Handling Challenges with Transparency and Solutions.** No real estate transaction is entirely without obstacles, and how agents handle challenges is a critical part of the service experience. When issues arise—whether related to financing, inspections, or negotiations—agents should address them honestly and promptly. Transparent communication during difficult moments reassures clients and helps maintain trust, even when setbacks occur.

   Equally important is the agent's approach to problem-solving. Rather than simply informing clients of an issue, agents should be prepared to offer solutions and alternatives. This proactive approach shows clients that their agent is dedicated to overcoming challenges and achieving the best possible outcome.

7. **Following Up After the Sale.** Managing the service experience does not end at closing. Following up with clients after the transaction demonstrates that the agent values the relationship beyond the immediate sale. A simple check-in to see how clients are settling into their new home, offering resources for local services, or

providing market updates can go a long way in strengthening the client-agent connection.

Post-sale engagement reinforces clients' positive experience with their agent, increasing the likelihood of referrals and future business. When clients feel supported even after the sale, they are more likely to view the transaction as a seamless, rewarding experience.

In today's evolving real estate landscape, transparency has become the cornerstone of effective buyer agency, transforming how agents engage with clients at every stage of the relationship. Key areas essential to successful buyer agency, include: (a) Building trust through open communication; (b) Transparent disclosure of agency compensation; (c) Adapting to changing buyer expectations in a transparent market; and (d) Managing buyer expectations and delivering a high-quality service experience.

We note that this chapter may appear to link transparency solely to compensation discussions (this is largely due to the focus on this area of transparency in the NAR litigation), but transparency in buyer agency is essential across many areas of a real estate transaction, including:

- **Agency Disclosure** – Clearly communicating your role and responsibilities as a buyer's agent and explaining agency relationships.

- **Property Condition** – Providing clients with honest, thorough information on property disclosures, inspections, and potential issues.

- **Market Data and Comparables** – Sharing accurate, up-to-date market data, including comparable sales, to help buyers make informed decisions.

- **Negotiation Tactics** – Being transparent about your negotiation strategy and explaining how it aligns with the buyer's goals.

- **Contract Terms and Conditions** – Explaining contract terms, contingencies, and deadlines to ensure buyers understand their obligations and options.

- **Financing Options** – Educating buyers on mortgage products, rates, and lender recommendations without bias.

- **Conflict of Interest Disclosure** – Disclosing any potential conflicts, such as relationships with other parties involved in the transaction.

- **Closing Costs and Fees** – Providing a detailed breakdown of anticipated closing costs and fees associated with the transaction.

- **Timeline Expectations** – Setting clear expectations for the transaction timeline and keeping clients updated on any changes.

- **Post-Purchase Obligations** – Informing buyers about any ongoing responsibilities, such as property maintenance, HOA rules, or future tax implications.

By focusing on all elements of transparency, agents can foster trust and meet the demands of today's informed buyers. By setting clear expectations, maintaining open communication, personalizing service, and handling challenges with transparency, agents can provide a seamless, client-centered experience that builds trust and loyalty. When agents prioritize the client's experience from start to finish, they not only meet but often exceed expectations, creating a foundation for long-term success and client satisfaction in today's dynamic real estate market. Embracing transparency is not just about adapting to new norms; it is about elevating the standard of service and building lasting relationships that benefit both clients and agents alike.

As buyer agency enters a new era, transparency has become the defining standard, reshaping client expectations and the agent's role. Navigating this new norm calls for a strategic approach, one that blends open communication with a strong foundation in client-centered practices. This is where the **P.I.E.R. Approach: Implementing Preparation, Innovation, Engagement & Retention to Attract and Retain Buyer Clients in This New Era of Real Estate**—comes into play. By redefining transparency and implementing these core principles, agents can build trust, meet evolving buyer demands, and deliver a seamless, high-quality service experience. The following chapter explores how to apply the

ERICKA L. DAVIS

P.I.E.R. Approach to thrive in a transparency-driven market and create lasting client relationships.

CHAPTER 3

The P.I.E.R. Approach: Using Preparation, Innovation, Engagement & Retention to Attract and Retain Buyer Clients in This New Era of Real Estate

The P.I.E.R. Approach Analogy

In a vast sea of prospective homebuyers, clients are searching for a solid PIER to help them safely dock on the shores of homeownership. Buyer's agents represent that P.I.E.R., guiding clients with a transparent, client-centered approach that ensures a secure and successful journey home.

In the previous chapter, we examined how redefining transparency has reshaped the landscape of buyer agency in the wake of the NAR Settlement. That discussion highlighted the core changes significantly impacting how agents interact with and serve clients. Now, we introduce the P.I.E.R. Approach—a four-part approach crafted to help buyer agents attract and retain clients in this evolving real estate environment to assist them in meeting their homeownership goals. This chapter offers actionable steps for implementing the P.I.E.R. Approach, equipping agents with a practical approach to thrive in the new, transparency-focused era of real estate.

The P.I.E.R. Approach centers on preparation, innovation, engagement, and retention—essential components in developing action plans that empower buyer agents to chart a tailored course for each client's success. In this chapter, we will break down each component of the P.I.E.R. Approach, equipping you with practical tools to integrate it effectively into your client's home-buying action plans.

PREPARATION

Preparation can be defined as building a strong foundation by understanding market changes, mastering transparent practices, and taking the initial steps to confidently articulate your value to clients. Preparation sets the stage for effective client interactions and service delivery. The preparation step is completed once a lead is secured but before an initial meeting. A lead often provides you with essential initial information, such as the client's name, desired home features, price range, preferred location, and financing status. Use this preliminary information to prepare for your initial meeting. If key details are missing, reach out with a call to gather the buyer's main preferences and confirm whether financing has been secured. With this information in hand, you can complete the preparation step effectively before your initial meeting.

1. **Building a Strong Foundation for Success in the Buyer Agency.** Preparation is a fundamental part of building a successful career as a buyer's agent. Preparation involves understanding market changes, mastering transparent practices, and confidently communicating value to clients. In a transparency-driven market, being well-prepared sets the foundation for effective client interactions and ensures that agents can deliver high-quality service tailored to the needs of today's informed buyers.

2. **Understanding market changes.** One of the core elements of preparation is staying informed about the latest market trends and regulatory changes. As recent shifts in real estate have introduced new norms for transparency, buyer agents need to understand how these changes affect their roles and responsibilities. By keeping up with market trends, agents can provide clients with accurate, timely information, whether it is about local property values, mortgage rates, or neighborhood growth. This awareness not only enables agents to give well-rounded advice but also helps them adapt to fluctuating market conditions, guiding clients more effectively through the buying process.

3. **Mastering transparent practices.** Preparation in a transparency-driven market requires shifting from traditional methods to transparent practices. Transparent practices also mean fully disclosing factors that impact a buyer's decision. From property histories and potential repair costs to neighborhood insights, sharing information openly allows clients to make well-informed choices. This transparency sets realistic expectations, ensuring that buyers feel confident and respected throughout the transaction. For agents, mastering these practices requires not only thorough preparation but also the ability to convey information in simple, non-technical language that resonates with clients.

4. **Articulating value with confidence.** Preparation is essential for articulating value effectively. A repeating theme in this book is that buyers with greater visibility into compensation structures want to see the direct benefits of the services they pay for. To meet these expectations, agents should be prepared to highlight their expertise, negotiation skills, and in-depth market knowledge. Preparation enables agents to confidently outline their role in each transaction stage, from property searches and

market analysis to contract negotiation and closing support.

Confidently articulating value also involves tailoring services to fit individual client needs. For instance, some buyers may prioritize comprehensive support, while others may seek a more cost-effective, a la carte approach. By being prepared to discuss different service levels and flexible fee options, agents can demonstrate their willingness to work within a buyer's budget without compromising on service quality. This flexibility shows that the agent understands the client's unique situation and is committed to creating a positive, customized experience.

5. **Setting the Stage for Effective Client Interactions.** Preparation paves the way for productive, trust-building client interactions. By understanding the market, mastering transparent practices, and articulating their value clearly, buyer agents can address client questions with confidence and clarity. This proactive approach sets a tone of professionalism and reliability, encouraging clients to engage openly and feel secure in their decisions. Effective client interactions also mean anticipating potential challenges and preparing solutions. Whether

addressing common concerns about fees, discussing the value of specific services, or guiding clients through competitive markets, a well-prepared agent can handle these situations seamlessly. Preparation helps agents become trusted advisors and proactive problem-solvers who provide reassurance in complex transactions.

Preparation is a proactive practice. It forms the backbone of success in buyer agency, especially in today's transparency-focused market. By staying informed about market changes, mastering transparent practices, and confidently articulating their value, agents build a strong foundation for effective service delivery. This preparation enables agents to forge trust-based relationships, meet evolving buyer expectations, and provide a client-centered experience that sets them apart. As a result, agents prioritizing preparation are well-positioned to thrive in an industry where adaptability, knowledge, and transparency are essential to lasting success.

With a solid foundation in place, the next step is to embrace innovation—leveraging new tools, technology, and flexible service models to meet the demands of today's informed buyers. By adopting innovative approaches, agents not only stand out but also align with the expectations of transparency and client-centered service, creating a competitive edge in a rapidly evolving market.

INNOVATION

Innovation is the action of introducing fresh ideas, methods, or products that add value, boost efficiency, or address existing challenges. It requires creativity and a readiness to challenge the status quo to improve processes, services, or products. Innovation can take the form of incremental improvements or disruptive changes that reshape an industry.

In real estate, innovation might mean adopting advanced technologies such as virtual property tours or CRM systems that streamline operations and enhance the client experience. It could also involve developing flexible service models tailored to clients' needs or leveraging data analytics to deliver personalized, insightful recommendations.

Innovation is the "I" in the P.I.E.R. Approach, representing the commitment to embrace new tools, technology, and service models that differentiate agents and meet the needs of today's informed buyers. By helping agents stand out and align with expectations for transparency and client-centered service, innovation becomes a key component in the preparation stage of the P.I.E.R. Buyer's agents can use innovative tools to effectively prepare and communicate a comprehensive home purchase plan to prospective clients.

1. **Leveraging tools, technology, and service models to excel in buyer agency.** In today's real estate market, innovation has become a crucial element of success, particularly for buyer agents navigating the demands of transparency and client-centered service. Embracing new tools, technology, and service models allows agents to set themselves apart while meeting the needs of increasingly informed and tech-savvy clients. Innovation is not just about adopting the latest trends—it is about strategically using advancements to improve service quality, enhance client trust, and create a streamlined experience that stands out in a competitive landscape.

2. **Adopting cutting-edge tools and technology.** Technology has transformed every industry, and real estate is no exception. Buyer agents who utilize the latest digital tools and platforms can deliver a seamless, data-driven experience that appeals to modern buyers. For example,

agents can use property search platforms that provide clients instant access to listings, neighborhood analytics, and market insights. This empowers buyers to make informed decisions and demonstrates an agent's commitment to transparency.

Tools like customer relationship management ("CRM") software also allow agents to track interactions, preferences, and transaction progress efficiently. A CRM system ensures that agents are proactive in following up with clients, responding to inquiries, and managing each phase of the buying process. Using CRM systems effectively, agents can tailor their approach to each client's needs, adding a personal touch that fosters trust and loyalty.

Virtual tools, such as video tours, 3D property walkthroughs, and virtual staging, have also become essential, especially in a market where clients prioritize convenience and flexibility. These tools allow buyers to view properties remotely, saving time and enhancing the experience. Virtual tours and digital property showcases also help buyers envision themselves in the space, which can be a deciding factor in a property search. By embracing these technologies, agents meet today's clients' demands and position themselves as forward-thinking professionals.

3. **Utilizing data analytics for client insights.** Another essential aspect of innovation is the ability to leverage data analytics to gain deeper insights into market trends and client preferences. By analyzing data on property sales, price trends, and buyer behavior, agents can provide clients with valuable insights that inform their purchasing decisions. For instance, understanding current market dynamics allows agents to advise clients on timing, pricing, and negotiation strategies, which can directly impact client satisfaction.

4. **Data analytics also helps agents anticipate client needs.** If an agent knows what properties a client has previously viewed or saved, they can recommend similar listings or highlight areas of interest. This level of personalization can set an agent apart by showing clients that they are paying attention to their unique preferences. With data-driven recommendations, agents can differentiate themselves as industry or niche experts who go beyond basic property searches to deliver value at every stage.

5. **Innovating with flexible service models.** In addition to technological innovation, adopting flexible service models is a key method to meet the needs of diverse buyers. Today's clients want options that fit their specific needs and financial situations. Agents offering varied service levels and fee structures are better positioned to attract and retain clients. This could mean offering a range of service packages, from full-service representation to more affordable a la carte options, such as negotiation support or transaction management.

By offering flexible service models, agents can cater to clients with varying budgets and preferences, which not only broadens their potential client base but also demonstrates adaptability. For example, some buyers prefer a comprehensive package covering every process step, while others opt for minimal assistance. Tailoring service models to fit client needs is an innovative approach that aligns with the demand for client-centered service, giving buyers more control over their investment in agent services.

6. **Enhancing transparency through technology.** Transparency has become a cornerstone of buyer agency,

and technology significantly facilitates this openness. Agents can use digital platforms to keep clients informed at every transaction stage, from initial property searches to closing. Online client portals, for instance, allow buyers to view documents, monitor transactions' progress, and receive updates in real-time. This level of transparency builds trust, as clients can see and understand every aspect of the process without feeling left in the dark.

Furthermore, online platforms can enable clients to compare properties, analyze investment potential, and access financial tools like mortgage calculators and cost estimators. When buyer agents make these resources readily available, they empower clients to take an active role in their home-buying journey. This technology-driven transparency improves the client experience and reinforces the agent's reputation as an ethical, client-centered professional.

7. **Positioning yourself as a client-centered innovator.** Innovation in real estate is not solely about using technology; it is about embracing a mindset that places the client at the center of every decision. Agents who prioritize innovation show a willingness to adapt and evolve with

their client's needs, which is essential for building lasting relationships. By positioning themselves as innovators, buyer agents demonstrate they are equipped to handle today's challenges and prepared to deliver solutions that enhance the overall client home purchase experience.

For example, agents can create value-added content—such as neighborhood guides, market insights, and educational webinars—that help clients make informed decisions. Sharing these resources shows clients that the agent is proactive, knowledgeable, and genuinely invested in their success. Additionally, by continuously seeking new ways to improve service delivery, agents reinforce their dedication to providing top-tier, client-focused service.

Innovation in the modern real estate landscape empowers buyer agents to stand out, establishing themselves as forward-thinking, client-centered professionals. By embracing new tools, data analytics, flexible service models, and enhanced transparency, agents lay a foundation for trust and success in a competitive market. However, innovation alone is not enough—agents must also focus on building meaningful, lasting connections with clients to ensure a truly exceptional experience. This brings us to the next essential component: engagement. Creating strong client relationships through open, ongoing communication and trust-building is key to delivering outstanding service and meeting the evolving needs of today's buyers.

ENGAGEMENT

Engagement creates meaningful connections with clients by fostering open, ongoing communication and building trust. Engagement strategies focus on understanding client needs, addressing concerns transparently, and maintaining a positive, responsive relationship. Communicating value in a transparent market is the art of developing innovative methods for articulating and justifying the value of buyer representation. Tips for discussing the unique benefits of a buyer agency, such as negotiation expertise, market knowledge, and guidance, to clients who are now more aware of costs.

1. **Building meaningful connections with clients in a transparent market.** In a market where transparency is the new standard, engagement is essential for buyer agents aiming to foster lasting client relationships. Engaging with

clients involves much more than simple communication—building trust, understanding client needs, and demonstrating value throughout the buying journey. By prioritizing engagement, agents can create meaningful connections through open, ongoing communication, addressing concerns transparently, and consistently showcasing the unique benefits of buyer representation.

2. **Building Trust Through Ongoing Communication.** Engagement begins with a commitment to open, consistent communication. In today's real estate market, buyers expect more than occasional updates; they want to feel informed and valued throughout every step of the process. Buyer agents who prioritize ongoing communication demonstrate reliability and transparency, essential elements that foster trust.

One effective way to enhance engagement is through regular check-ins and proactive updates. By reaching out with new market insights, relevant listings, or information on the progress of a transaction, agents keep clients in the loop and anticipate questions before they arise. This level of engagement reassures clients, showing that their agent is always one step ahead, providing information and support at each stage. Proactive engagement keeps clients informed and strengthens the client-agent relationship, as clients feel respected and cared for.

3. **Understanding client needs and addressing concerns transparently.** Genuine engagement requires a deep understanding of each client's unique needs, preferences, and concerns. Buyer agents who invest time in learning about their client's goals can tailor their services to create a more personalized experience. This client-centered approach reinforces the agent's role as a trusted advisor who listens to and prioritizes the buyer's interests.

To understand client needs fully, agents should ask open-ended questions during initial meetings and throughout the buying process. Questions like "What are your top priorities in a home?" or "How involved would you like to be in the decision-making process?" help agents gain insight into the client's expectations. Once these needs are understood, agents can address concerns and offer solutions transparently. For example, if a client worries about market competitiveness, an agent can explain strategies to navigate bidding wars or manage negotiation challenges. This level of transparency not only reassures clients but also helps them make informed decisions with confidence.

4. **Articulating and justifying the value of buyer representation.** In a transparent market, clients are more discerning and want to understand the tangible benefits of buyer representation. This is where the agent's role in articulating value becomes essential. To communicate value effectively, agents must go beyond listing services; they must explain why each service is beneficial and how it directly supports the client's goals.

One effective approach is to highlight the unique benefits of buyer agency, such as negotiation expertise, local market knowledge, and guidance throughout the transaction. Agents can provide examples of how these skills have made a difference in past transactions, such as helping clients secure a lower purchase price or navigating complex contract terms. By offering specific examples, agents demonstrate the real-world impact of their expertise, making it easier for clients to see the value of their investment.

Additionally, buyer's agents should emphasize their role in protecting the client's interests. Unlike listing agents, who represent the seller, buyer agents are dedicated solely to advocating for the buyer. This means providing honest advice, conducting thorough market research, and negotiating in the buyer's best interest. By clearly articulating this distinction, agents reinforce their commitment to helping clients achieve the best possible outcome, whether by securing favorable terms or avoiding costly pitfalls.

5. **Maintaining a Positive, Responsive Relationship.** Engagement does not end when an offer is accepted; it extends through the closing and beyond. Maintaining a positive, responsive relationship means supporting clients and promptly addressing any questions or concerns, even as the transaction nears completion. Simple gestures like regular check-ins, updates on closing milestones, and reminders about next steps show clients that their agent is fully committed to seeing the process through successfully.

After closing, agents can continue to engage clients by helping with post-purchase needs, such as recommending contractors, providing insights on property maintenance, or sending periodic market updates. This long-term engagement fosters client loyalty and increases the likelihood of referrals, as clients are more likely to recommend an agent who consistently provides value and support.

In today's transparent, client-centered real estate market, engagement is essential for building lasting, trust-based relationships. By prioritizing open communication, understanding client needs, and clearly articulating the value of buyer representation, agents can effectively meet the expectations of informed clients. This approach differentiates agents and reinforces their role as knowledgeable, trustworthy professionals. Through meaningful engagement, buyer agents create a positive client experience that extends beyond the transaction, establishing themselves as trusted advisors in an increasingly transparent market.

However, maintaining this level of client satisfaction requires consistent value and responsiveness to client feedback. This brings us to the next essential component: retention. Ensuring long-term client satisfaction involves cultivating loyalty through quality service, proactive follow-up, and a commitment to strong, trust-based relationships even after the transaction is complete. Achieving and sustaining this level of client satisfaction demands a continuous commitment to delivering value and actively responding to client feedback. This leads us to the next essential component of the P.I.E.R Approach, retention.

RETENTION

Retention is the act of ensuring long-term client satisfaction by consistently delivering value and adapting to client feedback. Retention involves cultivating loyalty through quality service, follow-up, and maintaining strong, trust-based relationships even after transactions are complete.

1. **Building long-term client satisfaction and loyalty in a buyer agency.** In real estate, client retention is just as important as client acquisition. Retaining clients leads to repeat business and drives valuable referrals, helping agents establish a reputation for reliability and trustworthiness. Retention requires more than transaction completion—it demands consistent value delivery, adaptability to client feedback, and a commitment to

maintaining relationships long after the deal is closed. By focusing on long-term client satisfaction, buyer agents can cultivate loyalty and position themselves as trusted advisors in an increasingly competitive and transparent market.

2. **Consistently Delivering Value.** Retention begins with a foundation of value. To retain clients, agents must demonstrate their commitment to quality service throughout the buying process and beyond. Every interaction with a client presents an opportunity to reinforce value, whether by offering insightful advice, responding to inquiries promptly, or ensuring that the transaction process is as smooth as possible.

Delivering consistent value also means personalizing the buying experience to meet each client's unique needs. When agents take the time to understand a client's goals, preferences, and concerns, they create a tailored experience that resonates and builds trust. This dedication to personalizing service helps clients feel valued, knowing that their agent is working in their best interest. By going above and beyond to provide high-quality, individualized service, agents lay the groundwork for lasting relationships.

3. **Adapting to client feedback.** Adapting to feedback is another essential aspect of retention. Today's clients expect agents to listen to and act on their input, whether it relates to communication preferences, service expectations, or specific transaction needs. Feedback gives agents valuable insights on how to improve their approach and better serve their clients.

Agents can actively seek feedback through surveys, post-transaction check-ins, or casual conversations. This approach shows clients that their opinions are valued and that the agent is committed to continuous improvement. For example, if a client desires more frequent updates during the search process, an agent can adjust their communication style accordingly. Agents demonstrate flexibility and dedication to enhancing the client experience by making changes based on client feedback. In addition to making immediate adjustments, agents can use feedback to refine their overall approach to buyer representation. Patterns in feedback may reveal areas for professional growth, such as improving negotiation skills, expanding market knowledge, or fine-tuning communication strategies. By adapting based on client insights, agents build a service model that is responsive, client-centered, and continually evolving.

4. **Cultivating Loyalty Through Follow-Up and Post-Transaction Support.** The relationship between an agent and a client does not end at closing. In fact, the post-transaction period is a critical time for building loyalty. By following up with clients after the sale and offering continued support, agents reinforce their commitment to client satisfaction and show that they value the relationship beyond a single transaction.

Follow-up can take various forms, from checking in to see how clients are settling into their new homes to offering resources and recommendations for home maintenance or improvements. Simple gestures demonstrate care and attention to detail, such as sending a handwritten note, providing a list of local service providers, or offering market updates on property values. These actions strengthen the client's impression of their agent as a dedicated, supportive professional.

Post-transaction support can also involve keeping clients informed about relevant market trends, which can be particularly valuable for buyers looking to monitor the appreciation of their property. By maintaining a positive, helpful relationship even after the sale, agents foster trust and increase the likelihood that clients will return to them for future transactions or refer them to friends and family.

5. **Building trust-based relationships.** Trust is the foundation of client retention, and agents who prioritize transparency, honesty, and integrity build relationships that stand the test of time. Trust-based relationships involve clear communication, realistic expectations, and ethical practices. When clients feel that their agent is acting in their best interests, they are more likely to return for future transactions and recommend them to others.

To cultivate trust, agents should remain accessible and responsive, addressing any questions or concerns openly. By being transparent about market conditions, property values, and transaction processes, agents empower clients to make informed decisions. Furthermore, agents who are proactive in identifying potential challenges and providing solutions demonstrate reliability, which strengthens the client's confidence in their expertise.

6. **Building trust-based relationships requires consistency.** Clients remember agents who are reliable, attentive, and knowledgeable, and these qualities contribute to a positive client experience. Even small acts, such as answering calls promptly or providing detailed property insights, contribute to a lasting impression of professionalism and dedication. By continuously reinforcing trust through honest, client-centered practices, agents build a foundation for long-term loyalty.

7. **The Role of Retention in a Competitive Market.** In a competitive real estate market, retention offers a distinct advantage. Agents who focus on retaining clients reduce their dependence on constant prospecting, as loyal clients are more likely to provide repeat business and referrals. Additionally, a client-centered approach to retention enhances the agent's reputation within the community. Satisfied clients often share their positive experiences, which can lead to new clients who have already heard of the agent's excellent service. Retention also allows agents to build a strong network of clients who trust their expertise

and judgment. Over time, these relationships create a valuable referral network that contributes to steady business growth. In a market where clients have more options than ever, agents who focus on retention differentiate themselves by demonstrating a commitment to lasting relationships and client satisfaction.

Retention is a cornerstone of success in buyer agency, ensuring that clients remain satisfied and loyal long after a transaction is complete. By consistently delivering value, adapting to client feedback, and offering follow-up support, agents can build meaningful, trust-based relationships that lead to repeat business and referrals. In a competitive market, client retention not only strengthens an agent's reputation but also creates a foundation for sustainable growth. For buyer agents, focusing on retention is more than completing transactions—it is about building lasting connections that benefit both the client and the agent for years to come.

The P.I.E.R. Approach—Preparation, Innovation, Engagement, and Retention—provides buyer agents with a comprehensive framework for success in today's real estate landscape. Each component of this approach works together to empower agents to meet the demands of transparency, build lasting client relationships, and deliver exceptional service.

Through **preparation**, agents lay a strong foundation by mastering market knowledge and transparent practices, setting the stage for trust and effective service. **Innovation** keeps agents competitive and responsive, helping them adapt to client needs in a rapidly evolving market. **Engagement** strengthens client connections with open, meaningful communication, ensuring clients feel supported and valued.

Lastly, **retention** secures long-term loyalty and satisfaction, creating a cycle of repeat business and referrals that drive sustained growth. The P.I.E.R. Approach enables buyer agents to confidently navigate the evolving expectations of today's buyers, reinforcing their roles as trusted advisors. By adopting this client-centered strategy, agents position themselves for lasting success in the dynamic, client-focused world of real estate.

The P.I.E.R. Approach—Preparation, Innovation, Engagement, and Retention—provides buyer agents with a structured framework for excelling in today's transparency-driven, client-centered real estate market. By preparing market insights, adopting innovative tools, fostering meaningful engagement, and prioritizing retention, agents can meet clients' evolving expectations and deliver an exceptional service experience that builds trust and loyalty. The P.I.E.R. Approach empowers agents to navigate a dynamic landscape confidently, setting the stage for long-term client relationships.

Reader Reflect and Review

Reflection. Write down one specific action you can take in each of the P.I.E.R. components (Preparation, Innovation, Engagement, Retention) to enhance your client relationships. Be as specific as possible.

_____

_____

_____

_____

_____

To deepen this client-centered strategy, we turn to the **Agency, Advocacy, and Advisory ... The Three 'A' Approach** in Buyer

Representation. This next chapter will explore how these foundational roles further reinforce the agent's value, guiding clients through every step of the home-buying journey with professionalism, support, and trusted expertise. Together, the P.I.E.R. and Three 'A' Approaches create a cohesive strategy for delivering the highest level of service in buyer agency and realty agency overall.

CHAPTER 4

Agency, Advocacy, and Advisory ... The Three 'A' Approach in Buyer Representation

The Three 'A' Approach in Buyer Representation

The process of buying a home is often complex, filled with critical decisions and moments that require expert guidance. To help buyers navigate this journey successfully, agents can employ the **Three 'A' Approach—Agency, Advocacy, and Advisory.** This method provides a structured, client-centered framework that builds trust, ensures effective representation, and delivers exceptional service tailored to the client's unique needs.

Agency: Representing the Buyer with Integrity and Professionalism

The first "A" in the Three 'A' Approach is **Agency**. Agency involves acting as a licensed representative who manages all aspects of the home-buying process while prioritizing the buyer's best interests. This role involves taking on the legal responsibility to act as the buyer's fiduciary, ensuring their needs are at the forefront of every decision and negotiation.

- **Defining Agency in Real Estate.** As agents, professionals serve as intermediaries who guide buyers through each step, from the initial property search to the final closing. The agency establishes a foundation of trust and reliability, as buyers know they have a dedicated professional advocating for their goals.

- **Responsibilities in Agency.** Key responsibilities include coordinating property showings, preparing and submitting offers, handling negotiation strategies, and managing paperwork. By taking charge of these logistical and legal elements, agents relieve buyers of stress and help them make decisions confidently.

- **Transparency and Communication.** Effective agency also requires transparent communication. Agents must clarify the details of the agency relationship, including compensation structures and potential conflicts of interest, so clients are fully informed from the outset.

Advocacy: Championing the Buyer's Needs and Goals

The second 'A,'" **Advocacy**, focuses on the agent's role as a proactive advocate for the buyer. This step goes beyond simply guiding the buyer through the process; it involves actively fighting for the buyer's best interests, whether in negotiations, property evaluations, or contract terms. Advocacy builds loyalty and trust, as buyers feel reassured knowing that their agent is fully committed to achieving their desired outcomes.

- **Understanding the Buyer's Goals.** Effective advocacy begins with understanding the buyer's priorities, whether it is finding a specific neighborhood, staying within budget, or securing certain amenities. By focusing on the client's unique needs, agents can tailor their strategies to meet these goals.

- **Negotiation and Problem-Solving.** Advocacy often means going to bat for the buyer during negotiations, using tactics to secure favorable terms or pricing. It also involves solving any issues that arise, such as addressing concerns from inspections, managing competitive bidding, or resolving contractual complications.

- **Protecting Buyer Interests.** Advocates monitor market conditions, property values, and contract fine details to ensure that clients are protected from potential risks. By advocating for fair terms and looking for red flags, agents reinforce their commitment to the buyer's success.

Advisory: Providing Strategic Guidance and Market Insights

The third 'A' **Advisory** is where agents add immense value by offering their expertise and market knowledge to guide buyers in making informed decisions. In today's data-driven and fast-paced real estate landscape, buyers benefit from an advisor who can interpret market trends, provide financial insights, and offer personalized advice.

- **Market Analysis and Insights.** Advisors analyze market conditions to help buyers understand local price trends, neighborhood dynamics, and overall investment potential. This knowledge enables buyers to make competitive offers and helps them identify properties that align with their financial and lifestyle goals.

- **Financial Guidance.** While agents are not financial advisors, they can offer insights on budgeting, financing options, and potential return on investment, empowering buyers to consider the long-term implications of their purchase. For example, advising buyers on how to structure an offer to remain within budget while still competitive.

- **Personalized Recommendations.** Advisors understand that each buyer has unique preferences, so they provide tailored recommendations on properties, neighborhoods, and buying strategies. Whether recommending schools in family-friendly neighborhoods or explaining the pros and cons of a property, advisors ensure buyers have all the information they need to proceed confidently.

Putting the Three 'A' Approach into Practice

Implementing the Three 'A' Approach requires skillful balance. Here's how agents can put each aspect into action to deliver an exceptional, client-centered experience:

- **Start with a Foundation of Agency.** Begin the relationship by explaining your role as an agent, including your fiduciary responsibilities and commitment to transparency. Outline the process, compensation structure, and your dedication to client advocacy.

- **Engage in Active Advocacy Throughout the Search.** Actively listen to your client's needs and ensure they know you are there to support and champion their interests. Reinforce your advocacy role by keeping their goals and protections at the forefront during negotiations or challenging situations.

- **Provide strategic advisory at key decision points.** Share market insights and property analysis and offer guidance on each critical decision. Offer recommendations grounded in data, local knowledge, and your experience, allowing clients to make informed, confident choices.

Benefits of the Three 'A' Approach

- **Builds Trust and Loyalty.** By consistently prioritizing the buyer's interests through agency, advocacy, and advisory, agents cultivate trust, creating loyal clients who will likely return for future transactions and provide referrals.

- **Enhances client satisfaction.** This approach ensures that clients feel supported, informed, and protected throughout the process, leading to a more satisfying experience and greater client retention.

- **Differentiates the Agent.** In a competitive market, the Three 'A' Approach sets agents apart as knowledgeable, proactive professionals who bring value and commitment to every client relationship.

The Three 'A' Approach—Agency, Advocacy, and Advisory—provides a powerful framework for buyer agents seeking a comprehensive, client-centered service. By acting as the buyer's trusted agent, proactive advocate, and knowledgeable advisor, agents can guide clients through the homebuying journey with confidence, integrity, and success. Embracing this approach enhances client satisfaction and establishes the agent as a trusted professional in a transparency-driven market. Through the Three 'A' Approach, agents can build meaningful, lasting relationships that create value for both their clients and their business.

P.I.E.R. Approach and the Three 'A' Approach as Complementary Strategies

The **P.I.E.R. Approach** and the **Three 'A' Approach**—**Agency, Advocacy, and Advisory** are complementary strategies that together create a robust framework for buyer agents to provide exceptional, client-centered service. Each element of the P.I.E.R. Approach aligns closely with the Three A principles, strengthening the agent's role as a knowledgeable, proactive, and trusted advisor.

- **Preparation and Agency.** The **preparation** component of P.I.E.R. strengthens the **agency** role by equipping agents with comprehensive knowledge and skills to represent their clients effectively. Agents fulfill their fiduciary duty and build trust as committed representatives by understanding market trends, reviewing properties, and setting clear expectations.

- **Innovation and Advisory. Innovation** aligns seamlessly with **Advisory** by enabling agents to leverage the latest tools, technologies, and flexible service models to offer valuable, data-driven insights. As trusted advisors, agents who innovate can provide clients with personalized, relevant information that enhances decision-making and highlights the agent's expertise in a competitive market.

- **Engagement and Advocacy. Engagement** closely connects with **Advocacy**, as both involve actively listening to client needs, fostering open communication, and supporting the client's interests throughout the process. By engaging meaningfully with clients, agents strengthen their role as advocates, ensuring clients feel informed, understood, and confident in each stage of the transaction.

- **Retention and Relationship Building**. Finally, **retention** extends the impact of **agency, advocacy, and advisory** by focusing on long-term client satisfaction. Retention builds loyalty through consistent follow-up, ongoing support, and reinforcing the agent's commitment to each client's success even after the transaction concludes.

The P.I.E.R. Approach and the Three 'A' Approach create a comprehensive strategy that enables buyer agents to deliver high-value, transparent, and personalized service. By aligning these frameworks, agents can establish themselves as trusted, adaptable, and client-focused professionals prepared for long-term success in the real estate industry.

CHAPTER 5

"To the Time Machine!" Buyer Agency in 2025 and Beyond, Preparing for the Future of Real Estate

… ERICKA L. DAVIS

Buyer Agency in 2025 and Beyond, Preparing for the Future of Real Estate

As the real estate industry evolves, agency is undergoing significant transformations, reshaped by transparency, technology, and shifting client expectations. To succeed in 2025 and beyond, buyer agents must keep pace with these changes and prepare for emerging trends that will redefine their roles and relationships with clients. This chapter equips agents when supporting buyers with insights and tools to stay ahead, adapt to industry changes, and ensure a sustainable career in the future of real estate.

Adapting to a Transparency-Driven Market

Transparency has become a cornerstone of modern real estate, especially with the recent NAR Settlement, which mandates clearer disclosures around compensation and service offerings. As transparency becomes the norm, buyer agents must be prepared to communicate openly about their fees, service structures, and the value they provide to clients.

- **Clear Fee Disclosures.** In 2025, agents should expect clients to have greater insight into commission structures and service fees. Agents must be comfortable discussing fees upfront and justifying their value to build trust.

- **Transparent Service Offerings.** Beyond fee transparency, agents should provide clients with a clear understanding of the services included in buyer representation, whether through tiered service packages or custom options. This clarity helps clients make informed decisions and builds trust.

- **Building a Reputation for Integrity.** As clients increasingly seek ethical and client-centered agents, maintaining a reputation for honesty, fairness, and integrity will be essential for long-term success.

Embracing Technological Advancements

Technology is accelerating changes in real estate, and by 2025, buyer agents will rely more heavily on digital tools and platforms to enhance the client experience and streamline operations. From virtual tours to AI-driven property search tools, embracing technology will be crucial for agents aiming to remain competitive.

- **Virtual and Augmented Reality.** Virtual property tours, 3D walkthroughs, and augmented reality features will become more prevalent, allowing clients to explore properties remotely. Agents should familiarize themselves with these technologies to offer a more convenient and immersive client experience.

- **Artificial Intelligence and Data Analytics.** AI-driven tools can provide valuable insights into market trends, pricing predictions, and buyer preferences, enabling agents to offer personalized recommendations. By leveraging data analytics, agents can more accurately identify client needs and preferences, enhancing the decision-making process.

- **Digital Transaction Management.** Digital platforms that manage contracts, paperwork, and compliance will streamline the buying process, making it more efficient for clients and agents. Familiarity with these tools will help agents improve productivity and maintain a high standard of service.

Focusing on Personalized Client Experiences

As technology empowers buyers with more information, clients expect a personalized, client-centered approach. Buyer agents must focus on creating tailored experiences that cater to each client's unique needs and goals.

- **Customizable Service Packages.** Offering flexible service options allows clients to choose the level of support they need based on their budget and preferences. By creating packages that address different service levels, agents can cater to a wider variety of clients while providing transparency on what each option includes.

- **Data-Driven Personalization.** Using data analytics, agents can anticipate client needs and preferences and send relevant listings, neighborhood insights, and market updates. This level of personalization shows clients that their agent understands and values their individual goals.

- **High-Quality Communication.** As clients become more accustomed to immediate access to information, agents must prioritize timely, proactive communication. Regular updates, follow-ups, and transparency at each stage of the transaction are essential for a seamless client experience.

Prioritizing Ethical Standards and Professional Growth

In an era where clients value ethical standards and professionalism, buyer agents must prioritize ongoing education and ethical practices to remain relevant and respected. Agents who demonstrate a commitment to integrity and continuous improvement will have a competitive edge in a rapidly changing industry.

- **Commitment to Ethical Practices.** Transparency in fees, honest representation, and full disclosure are more important than ever in building client trust. Agents should stay updated on ethical guidelines and consistently apply them to their practices.

- **Continual Professional Development.** With ongoing changes in technology, market conditions, and legal requirements, agents must prioritize continued education to keep their skills sharp. Agents can better serve clients and respond to new challenges by staying informed about industry trends.

- **Building a client-centered reputation.** As buyers increasingly seek agents with strong ethical standards, developing a reputation as a client-centered professional will be key to long-term success. Agents who prioritize ethical practices, transparent communication, and a commitment to client satisfaction will stand out.

Preparing for Future Market Trends and Client Expectations

Buyer agents will need to adapt to a continually shifting landscape driven by economic changes, demographic shifts, and evolving client expectations. By anticipating these trends, agents can position themselves as forward-thinking advisors prepared to guide clients through future market conditions.

- **Adapting to Economic Conditions.** Economic fluctuations and changing interest rates may affect buyer behavior. Agents should stay informed about economic trends to advise clients on the best timing and strategies for buying in uncertain markets.

- **Serving Millennial and Gen Z Buyers.** As Millennials and Gen Z increasingly enter the housing market, their preferences—such as sustainable living, technology integration, and flexible workspaces—will influence demand. Agents should understand the unique needs of these generations to provide relevant services.

- **Planning for Long-Term Client Relationships.** The future of buyer agency is not just about closing deals but about building long-term relationships. Agents who prioritize retention by staying connected with clients after the transaction and providing ongoing value will foster loyalty and create a steady referral network.

Anticipate Future Legal Developments

The 2024 National Association of Realtors settlement has introduced significant changes to real estate practices, particularly concerning buyer agency. While the settlement aims to enhance transparency and fairness, it also presents ongoing legal challenges that could further impact the industry.

- **Continued Antitrust Scrutiny.** Despite the settlement, the real estate sector remains under antitrust scrutiny. The U.S. Department of Justice ("DOJ") has expressed interest in investigating NAR's practices beyond the terms of the settlement. In October 2024, NAR petitioned the U.S. Supreme Court to block a DOJ probe, arguing that it violates a prior agreement. The outcome of this legal battle could lead to further regulatory changes affecting buyer agency practices.

- **Objections to Settlement Terms.** As the settlement approaches final approval, various objections have emerged. Some stakeholders argue that the settlement's nationwide scope is too broad and may preclude claims in other lawsuits. Others contend that the business practice changes and attorneys' fees outlined in the settlement are inadequate or unfair. These objections could result in modifications to the settlement terms or additional legal proceedings, influencing how buyer agents operate.

- **Future Legal Developments.** The real estate industry should anticipate additional legal developments as courts and regulatory bodies address the complexities arising from the settlement. These may include new guidelines on commission disclosures, adjustments to MLS policies, and further antitrust investigations. Buyer agents must stay informed about these changes to ensure compliance and adapt their practices accordingly.

- **Preparing for ongoing changes.** To navigate the evolving legal landscape, buyer agents should:
    - **Stay Informed.** Regularly monitor legal developments and industry news to remain aware of changes that could affect their practices.

    - **Seek Legal and/or Professional Counsel.** Consult with legal professionals or industry regulators to understand the implications of new regulations and ensure compliance.

    - **Adapt Business Models.** Be prepared to adjust commission structures and service offerings in response to legal requirements and market expectations.

By proactively addressing these challenges, buyer agents can continue to provide valuable services while adhering to the evolving legal standards in the real estate industry.

Putting It All Together: A Strategic Vision for 2025 and Beyond

The future of buyer agency requires a proactive, adaptable approach. Agents can build a resilient and successful career by combining transparency, technology, personalized service, ethical practices, and an understanding of future trends. Here is a strategic summary to guide buyer agents as they navigate this evolving landscape:

- **Implement a Client-Centered Transparency Approach.** Make transparency a foundational practice, from fee disclosures to clear service explanations. This builds trust and aligns with client expectations.

- **Embrace and Integrate Technology.** Utilize cutting-edge tools like virtual tours, AI, and data analytics to provide an enhanced, efficient service experience that meets the demands of today's informed buyers.

- **Focus on Personalized Experiences.** Offer customizable service options and tailor communication to each client's unique needs, reinforcing the value of buyer representation.

- **Commit to Ethics and Professional Development.** Uphold ethical standards and invest in continued learning to remain competitive and respected in an ever-evolving market.

- **Anticipate and Adapt to Future Trends.** Stay informed about market shifts, changing demographics, and new buyer preferences to position yourself as a knowledgeable, future-ready advisor.

- **Foresee Future Legal Developments.** As courts and regulatory bodies address the complexities stemming from the settlement, anticipate additional legal developments.

As the buyer agency moves into 2025 and beyond, agents who proactively embrace transparency, technological advancements, and evolving client expectations will be positioned for lasting success. By focusing on transparency, innovation, ethical standards, and personalized service, buyer agents can cultivate trust-based relationships that foster long-term satisfaction and career resilience. In a future where clients have more choices and access to information, agents who prioritize adaptability, integrity, and a client-centered approach will emerge as leaders in the real estate industry.

However, the 2024 National Association of Realtors settlement introduced ongoing legal considerations that may continue to shape industry practices, particularly around buyer agency. While this settlement aims to improve transparency and fairness, it also opens the door to further legal challenges, potentially leading to additional regulatory adjustments, practice changes, and market impacts. By staying informed and prepared for these developments, buyer agents can navigate the evolving legal landscape effectively, ensuring compliance and sustained success in an increasingly competitive real estate environment.

Now that you have explored the legal challenges, approaches, and themes shaping the future of buyer agency, are you ready to make the choice to Quit or Pivot? The following chapter will offer a pros and cons analysis to guide you through this decision-making process. Let us dive deeper into the factors at play as we examine **The Decision... to Quit or Pivot. Making Career Decisions in the Post-Settlement Landscape.**

CHAPTER 6

The Decision... to Quit or Pivot? Making Career Decisions in the Post-Settlement Landscape

ERICKA L. DAVIS

Making Career Decisions in the Post-Settlement Landscape

In the wake of sweeping industry changes following the 2024 NAR Settlement, buyer agents face critical choices regarding their career paths. This chapter is an exercise that will equip buyer agents with reflection, knowledge, and resources to make informed, confident career decisions. Whether you decide to quit, pivot, adapt, or explore new roles, the exercises within this chapter will provide valuable insight into making choices that align with your strengths, goals, and the evolving landscape of buyer agency. By examining each section below and thoughtfully using their career thermometer, agents can align their career choices with their values, strengths, and long-term goals.

This text provides a reflection-forward exercise to assist you in making a decision that aligns with your personal and professional interests. It aims to empower agents to make informed, confident career choices that align with their strengths, aspirations, and the evolving landscape of buyer agency. Take your time to reflect deeply and consider discussing your thoughts with trusted colleagues, mentors, or a career advisor as you delve into your experience and decide to quit, pivot, or redefine your career in real estate.

SECTION 1. Assessing the Impact of the NAR Settlement on Your Career

Understanding Changes to Transparency and Compensation. This section will help you analyze the settlement's impact on transparency and compensation requirements, specifically how these changes redefine the role of buyer agents. By understanding the effects of these shifts on day-to-day practices, you can evaluate if they align with your career aspirations and values. By examining how these transparency and compensation changes influence your daily responsibilities, this section will help you assess whether the evolving expectations of a buyer's agency align with your professional goals and personal values.

Evaluating Career Alignment. Assess whether the new requirements in transparency and compensation align with your personal and professional goals. For those motivated by client-centered, transparent practices, these changes may reinforce their career path, while others may find that these requirements create misalignment.

Section Reflection One. In a buyer agency capacity, reflect on and identify specific adjustments that you have made in your approach since the 2024 NAR Settlement went into effect. By focusing on the unique steps added to your practices, as a buyer's agent, you can assess how you are individually meeting the new standards of transparency, compensation negotiation, and client-centered service. Here are some guiding thoughts to assist you with exploring this prompt:

A. Transparent Compensation Discussions:
- ☐ Have you implemented a structured approach to explaining your fees and services?
- ☐ Do you now include a specific discussion on commission breakdowns in initial client meetings?

B. Enhanced Documentation and Communication:
- ☐ Are there new documents or forms you have started using to meet disclosure requirements?

- ☐ Have you adopted new communication techniques, like visual aids or breakdowns, to help clients understand costs and services better?

C. **Client Education and Engagement:**
- ☐ How have you adjusted your educational practices? Are you providing more information upfront regarding compensation and the agent's role?
- ☐ Do you now spend more time discussing the value of representation and answering questions about fees?

D. **Customized Service Packages:**
- ☐ Have you developed new service tiers or packages to give clients more choice and control over their experience?
- ☐ How are you presenting these options and explaining their benefits?

Reflecting on these unique steps allows you, as an agent, to see how you are adapting effectively and identify areas where further adjustments might benefit your real estate practice.

SECTION 2. Evaluating Your Skills and Strengths

Identifying High-Value Skills in a Changing Market. Learn how to assess which of your skills are most relevant in the current landscape. Whether it is your negotiation expertise, market knowledge, or adaptability, you will explore ways to leverage your strengths to navigate this new landscape effectively.

Leveraging Your Core Competencies. This section also provides insights into maximizing your unique skills—whether through adapting to the new transparency demands or exploring alternative career avenues where your talents may be more aligned.

Section Reflection Two. Take a moment to reflect on the skills that set you apart in today's evolving real estate market. Consider how these abilities can help you thrive amidst new industry demands and increased transparency expectations.

A. Identify Your High-Value Skills:

- ☐ List the top skills you bring to your role as a buyer's agent (e.g., negotiation expertise, local market knowledge, client communication).
- ☐ For each skill, reflect on how it helps you navigate the current landscape.
- ☐ *Example question: How does my negotiation expertise enhance my ability to meet new transparency and client-centered requirements?*

B. Evaluate the Relevance of Your Skills in the Changing Market:
- ☐ Assess how relevant each skill is in today's real estate environment.
- ☐ Consider any areas where you may need to adapt or acquire new skills to stay competitive.
- ☐ *Example Question: Which of my skills will help me stand out most in a market that values transparency and flexible compensation?*

C. Leverage Your Core Competencies:
- ☐ Think about ways you can maximize these skills to add value to your clients and differentiate yourself from competitors.

- ☐ Reflect on how these core competencies can support you in adapting to the new demands of transparency or in exploring alternative real estate roles.
- ☐ *Example question: How can I use my adaptability to meet transparency expectations and potentially develop new service offerings?*

D. **Consider Opportunities for Growth:**
- ☐ Identify any areas for skill development that may enhance your ability to succeed in a changing market.
- ☐ Reflect on how expanding your competencies could open doors to new opportunities or alternative career avenues.
- ☐ *Example question: What additional skills would help me leverage my strengths more effectively in a transparency-driven environment?*

SECTION 3. Exploring New Career Paths in Real Estate

Discovering Alternative Roles within the Industry. For those considering a shift, this section provides insight into various career paths within real estate that might be more fulfilling.

Options include roles in real estate consulting, agent training, marketing, or specializing in niche areas, each offering potential pathways in the post-settlement era.

Finding Fulfillment in New Avenues. Explore roles that maintain your industry connections while offering different professional experiences, such as working with investor clients, specializing in eco-friendly properties, or entering real estate technology.

Section Reflection Three. As the real estate landscape changes, it may be beneficial to explore alternative roles within the industry that align more closely with your skills, values, and career goals. Use this prompt to reflect on potential new avenues that could provide professional fulfillment while keeping you connected to the real estate field.

A. **Consider Alternative Roles in Real Estate:**
- ☐ Reflect on other areas within real estate that have caught your interest, such as consulting, agent training, marketing, or a specialized niche.
- ☐ Think about how your existing skills could transfer to these roles.

- *Example Question: Which alternative roles within real estate would allow me to utilize my current strengths while offering new challenges?*

B. Identify Fulfillment Factors:
- Consider what you value most in a career: is it client interaction, strategic planning, flexibility, or something else?
- Explore how different roles might fulfill these values.
- *Example Question: What aspects of my work bring me the most satisfaction, and which roles in real estate would allow me to focus more on these areas?*

C. Explore niche areas and specializations:
- Identify any niche areas that align with your interests, such as eco-friendly properties, real estate technology, or investor relations.
- Reflect on the potential growth opportunities and job satisfaction each niche might offer.
- *Example Question: How might specializing in a niche area, like sustainable properties or real estate technology, align with my long-term goals and bring added value to clients?*

D. **Assess the skills needed for new paths:**
- ☐ For each role or niche that interests you, consider whether additional skills or certifications are required.
- ☐ Reflect on your willingness and readiness to acquire these skills and what it might mean for your career.
- ☐ *Example Question: What new skills would I need to develop for a successful transition to a role in real estate consulting, agent training, or a specialized niche?*

E. **Evaluate Industry Connection and Stability:**
- ☐ Consider whether each new path would allow you to maintain strong industry connections and provide a stable, rewarding career.
- ☐ Think about the long-term potential of each role and how it fits into your vision of success.
- ☐ *Example Question: How does this new role align with my desire for professional growth and stability in the real estate industry?*

Reflecting on these questions can help you determine which alternative paths in real estate might offer you a fulfilling and sustainable career while allowing you to adapt to the industry's evolving demands.

SECTION 4. Steps for Pivoting Successfully

Strategies for Adapting Your Approach. For agents choosing to pivot rather than quit, this section covers actionable steps for adapting, including targeted continuing education, exploring new service offerings, and deepening specialization to meet client needs.

Developing a client-centered, niche-focused practice. Learn how to pivot by carving out a niche or rebranding your services to cater to specific client segments, such as first-time buyers, luxury clients, or tech-savvy buyers seeking transparent, data-driven guidance.

Section Reflection Four. If you are considering a pivot within your real estate career, use this exercise to reflect on the strategies that can help you adapt and create a more specialized, client-centered practice.

A. **Identify areas for skill development and education:**
  - ☐ Reflect on areas where additional training or continuing education could enhance your ability to meet clients' evolving needs.

- ☐ Consider any certifications or advanced courses that might help you stand out in a changing market.
- ☐ *Example Question: What new skills or knowledge could strengthen my client approach and position me as a trusted advisor in this evolving landscape?*

B. **Explore New Service Offerings:**
- ☐ Think about ways you could expand your service offerings to provide more value. Are there new or customized services you could add to meet specific client needs?
- ☐ Reflect on how these services could differentiate your practice and attract new clients.
- ☐ *Example question: What additional services could I offer to provide more value and cater to my client's unique needs?*

C. **Define Your Niche:**
- ☐ Identify specific client segments that resonate with your skills and interests, such as first-time buyers, luxury clients, or environmentally conscious buyers.
- ☐ Reflect on how focusing on a niche could enhance your brand and allow you to deliver highly tailored service.

- *Example Question: Which client segment aligns best with my strengths and interests, and how can I position myself as a go-to agent in this niche?*

D. **Rebrand Your Services for a client-centered approach:**
- Consider how you can reframe your services to appeal directly to your target audience. Think about branding, messaging, and communication strategies that highlight your client-centered approach.
- Reflect on how you could enhance transparency, data-driven insights, or personalization in your offerings to attract your ideal clients.
- *Example question: How can I rebrand my services to display my commitment to client satisfaction and differentiate myself from my competitors?*

E. **Set Goals for Your Pivot Strategy:**
- Outline actionable goals for your pivot, whether they involve gaining new clients in a niche market, increasing service offerings, or achieving a new certification.
- Reflect on how each goal aligns with your long-term vision and will meaningfully support your transition.

- *Example Question: What specific goals will help me successfully pivot and build a more focused, sustainable practice?*

F. **Evaluate challenges and solutions:**
   - Consider any challenges you might encounter in your pivot, such as competition, marketing adjustments, or client expectations.
   - Reflect on strategies or resources you could use to overcome these challenges and stay motivated in your new direction.
   - *Example Question: What obstacles might arise in my pivot, and how can I prepare to address them effectively?*

By exploring these questions, you will gain insight into the steps required for a successful pivot and be better equipped to adapt your practice to align with your strengths, values, and the needs of today's clients.

SECTION 5. Knowing When to Quit

Identifying Signs, It is Time for a Career Change. Recognize the indicators that may signal it is time to move on, including feeling out of alignment with the new norms of transparency and negotiation or finding the market's evolving demands unsustainable.

Exploring New Career Options Outside of Buyer Agency. For those who feel that staying in the buyer's agency no longer aligns with their goals, this section offers suggestions for transitioning into other roles, either within or outside of real estate, which may offer a better fit.

Section Reflection Five. Recognizing When It is Time to Move on from Buyer Agency

Use this exercise to assess whether continuing as a buyer agent aligns with your professional and personal goals. Reflect on the signs that may indicate it is time to transition and explore other career options that might better suit your values and aspirations.

A. **Evaluate Your Alignment with Industry Changes:**
- ☐ Reflect on how recent shifts in transparency and compensation negotiation impact your daily work. Do these changes feel aligned with your values, or do they create discomfort or stress?

- *Example Question: How do the new norms of transparency and compensation negotiation make me feel about my role as a buyer agent?*

B. **Assess your job satisfaction and motivation:**
   - Think about your current levels of job satisfaction, energy, and enthusiasm for your work. Have you noticed any decrease in motivation or increased frustration with client expectations or market demands?
   - *Example Question: Am I feeling as motivated and fulfilled by my work as I once did, or am I finding the market's evolving demands unsustainable?*

C. **Identify signs of Burnout or Misalignment:**
   - Reflect on any physical or mental signs of burnout, such as exhaustion, stress, or a feeling of disconnect from the industry. Note any recurring thoughts about leaving or dissatisfaction with industry norms.
   - *Example Question: Are there specific aspects of my role that cause ongoing frustration or feelings of misalignment with my personal and professional values?*

D. **Explore Alternative Career Paths:**
   - ☐ Consider roles outside of buyer agency that might align more closely with your strengths, interests, and values. Reflect on areas within or outside real estate where you could find fulfillment, such as consulting, property management, marketing, or education.
   - ☐ *Example Question: What career options could allow me to leverage my skills while offering a work environment more suited to my current needs and goals?*

E. **Assess Potential Benefits of a Career Change:**
   - ☐ Reflect on how a change in career direction might positively impact your work-life balance, mental well-being, or professional satisfaction.
   - ☐ *Example Question: How might transitioning into a different role benefit my personal and professional growth, well-being, and sense of purpose?*

F. **Set Goals for Exploring a New Path:**
   - ☐ If you are considering a transition, outline your next steps for exploring new career opportunities. This could include networking, researching roles, or gaining certifications relevant to a new path.

☐ *Example Question: What steps can I take to explore a potential career change in a way that feels manageable and motivating?*

Reflecting on these questions can help you determine whether staying in a buyer agency aligns with your goals or if a career change might offer a more fulfilling path forward. Trust your instincts as you evaluate this decision, and remember that finding the right professional fit is essential to long-term success and satisfaction.

SECTION 6. Making a confident decision

Tools for Decision-Making. This section provides frameworks, tools, and reflection exercises to help you decide between quitting, pivoting, or redefining your role in real estate. By evaluating both your strengths and aspirations, you can gain clarity on which path to pursue.

Building Confidence in Your Choice. This section includes strategies for building confidence in your decision, whichever path you choose. Whether you are staying in a buyer agency, pivoting to new service offerings, or transitioning to a new career, this section empowers you to move forward with certainty.

Section Reflection Six. This exercise aims to assist you in making a clear and confident decision regarding your future in real estate. Use it to evaluate your strengths, aspirations, and options as you consider whether to stay with the buyer agency, pivot to a new approach, or transition to a different career path.

A. **Reflect on Your Strengths and Aspirations:**
- ☐ Identify your key strengths and how they contribute to your success as a buyer's agent. Consider how these strengths align with your long-term career aspirations.
- ☐ *Example Question: Which of my strengths bring me the most satisfaction, and how do they fit into my ideal career path?*

B. **Consider Your Current Career Fit:**
- ☐ Reflect on whether buyer agency currently aligns with your professional values, personal goals, and daily job satisfaction. Think about what aspects of your role you enjoy most and which feel misaligned.

- *Example question: Does my role as a buyer agent fulfill my professional goals and values, or do I feel drawn toward a new direction?*

C. **Explore Your Options: Quit, Pivot, or Redefine:**
   - Take time to consider each possible path—staying in buyer agency, pivoting to a niche focus or different service model, or transitioning to a new career. List the potential benefits and challenges of each option.
   - *Example Question: What are the pros and cons of staying in my current role, pivoting to a new focus, or transitioning to a different field?*

D. **Visualize the outcomes:**
   - Envision how each decision would impact your daily life, professional satisfaction, and long-term goals. Reflect on which outcome aligns best with your vision for the future.
   - *Example Question: Which decision brings me the most excitement, fulfillment, and confidence for the future?*

E. **Identify Resources for Building Confidence:**
   - List any tools or resources—such as professional development courses, mentorship, or networking

groups—that could support your chosen path and help you build confidence in your decision.

- [ ] *Example Question: What resources can I rely on to support my decision and enhance my confidence in this new direction?*

F. Set Intentions for Moving Forward:

- [ ] Outline your next steps based on your chosen path, whether that involves developing new skills, researching alternative roles, or deepening your expertise in buyer agency. Set clear intentions to guide your transition.
- [ ] *Example question: What specific actions will help me move forward confidently with my decision and create a successful transition?*

G. Affirm Your Choice:

- [ ] Reflect on why your choice feels right for you and affirm your commitment to this path. Revisit your strengths and aspirations and acknowledge the positive impact this decision will have on your career and well-being.
- [ ] *Example Question: What makes me feel confident in this decision, and how will it help me reach my personal and professional goals?*

By thoughtfully working through these questions, you can make a confident, well-informed decision about your future in real estate, with a clear understanding of how each path aligns with your strengths, values, and aspirations.

The decision to quit or pivot in the post-settlement landscape of the real estate industry is a pivotal one that requires thoughtful self-reflection, assessment of industry changes, and alignment with personal goals. For buyer agents, this moment presents an opportunity to redefine success, whether by embracing new approaches within the agency, exploring specialized niches, or transitioning to alternative roles within or outside of real estate. By evaluating their strengths, considering client needs, and envisioning the future they desire, agents can make confident, purposeful decisions. Whether choosing to stay, pivot, or transition, those who approach this decision with clarity and intention will be well-prepared to thrive in an industry that values adaptability, transparency, and client-centered service.

CLOSING

In business," to pivot" refers to making a strategic shift or adjustment in direction to adapt to new conditions, goals, or challenges. This shift can involve changing one's approach, focus, or services while leveraging existing strengths and resources to meet evolving demands. "Pivoting" means staying flexible and proactive, ensuring continued relevance and success in a changing landscape. After reading this definition, ...

Now, does the phrase "to pivot" perfectly capture the shift required of real estate agents deciding to continue practicing in this ever-changing landscape.

This book was written to bring real estate agents into a conversation that has largely focused on legal nuances and consumer interests, often overlooking the required pivot that is mandatory from the agent's perspective. While this text primarily addresses buyer agency, many of its themes and strategies can be applied to the broader practice of real estate. The emphasis on buyer agency stems from a consumer perception that buyer agents' actions have sometimes appeared opaque, potentially overshadowing the goals of the clients they serve. Not only consumers but also real estate agents across the industry embrace the need for improved transparency for all stakeholders.

Real estate practices have not seen significant person-to-person changes since the advent of technology, which has streamlined existing processes rather than fundamentally altering agent-client interactions. However, the NAR litigation and its eventual settlement have brought about a shift that demands a deeper transformation—a renewal of transparency and clarity in agent practices. It is an opportunity for agents, whether they represent buyers or sellers, to embrace innovation in their approach. Those who adapt and grow in response to this change will become the bedrock of a new foundation in the real estate industry.

I hope this text has provided valuable guidance as you evaluate your current position and future direction in your career amidst recent industry changes. With preliminary tools to help you decide whether to adapt, specialize, or transition, this resource is designed to support you in aligning your knowledge with the evolving topics in real estate. The thematic summary below is intended to offer a clear review, helping you stay engaged and motivated in the ever-changing practice of real estate.

1. **Assessing the Impact of the NAR Settlement on Your Career:** Understanding how the new transparency and compensation requirements affect your role and evaluating whether these changes align with your career goals.

2. **Evaluating Your Skills and Strengths:** Identify which of your skills are most valuable in the evolving market and explore ways to leverage them, whether you choose to adapt or move in a new direction.

3. **Implementing strategic approaches to add value.** Integrate strategic approaches that allow agents to enhance their services, differentiate themselves in the market, and exceed client expectations.

4. **Exploring New Career Paths in Real Estate:** Insight into alternative real estate roles, such as consulting, training, or specialization, that might offer fulfillment in the post-settlement environment.

5. **Steps for Pivoting Successfully:** Strategies for agents choosing to adapt their approach, including continuing education, niche specialization, and developing new service offerings.

6. **Knowing When to Quit:** signs that a career change might be the best option, including when the new norms of transparency and negotiation no longer align with your values or goals.

7. **Making a Confident Decision:** Tools and frameworks for confidently deciding to quit, pivot, or redefine your career within a buyer's agency or other real estate areas.

This book was published before the final court approval of the National Association of Realtors ("NAR") settlement, scheduled for November 26, 2024.

USEFUL APPENDICES

APPENDIX I. What Should I Say?

Useful Scripts for Buyer Agency in the Post-Settlement Era of Real Estate

Here are some sample buyer agency scripts tailored to the new norms introduced by the NAR Settlement. These scripts address key areas, such as fee transparency, negotiating services, and communicating value to clients in a transparent and client-centered manner.

Script One. Initial Consultation: Setting Expectations on Fees and Services

Agent: "Thank you for considering me as your buyer's agent. Since recent changes in the industry emphasize transparency, I want to be upfront about how my fees work. Unlike in the past, buyer agent fees are now part of our direct agreement and may be discussed separately from the property price."

Client: "What does that mean for me as the buyer?"

Agent: "It means you'll have clear visibility on what you're investing in for buyer representation. We will outline a fee that reflects the services and expertise I bring to help you find the right home and negotiate the best possible terms. My goal is to ensure you have a seamless and rewarding buying experience, and I'm here to guide you through each step."

Script Two. Discussing Value and Services with a Client

Agent: "As your buyer's agent, I bring in-depth market knowledge, negotiation expertise, and support through every stage of the buying process. I'll handle research, coordinate viewings, and provide you with insights that will help you make the best possible decision."

Client: "How is this different from what other agents offer?"

Agent: "My approach is personalized to your needs, and I focus on transparency. If you would like, I can break down the specific services I offer and any fees associated with each so you will know exactly what to expect. This approach helps us customize my representation to match what matters most to you in a home purchase."

Script Three. Handling Objections about Fees

Client: "I noticed that buyer agents' fees are more visible now, and I've seen some agents offering discounts. Why should I pay a higher fee for your services?"

Agent: "I completely understand. The recent changes allow you to see more of the cost upfront, which I believe benefits both of us. My fee reflects the experience, resources, and attention I provide to each client, especially in areas like negotiating better terms, handling paperwork efficiently, and addressing any issues that arise. This service level often saves clients' money and stress in the long run."

Client: "So you think the added services are worth it?"

Agent: "Yes, and I'm confident in the value I bring. However, I want you to feel comfortable with your decision, so we can discuss any adjustments or specific services you might prioritize to align with your budget and needs."

Script Four. Script for Negotiating Fee Structure with Client

Agent: "As we move forward, I want to ensure we're aligned on the fee structure and what you'll receive in return. We have a few options: a standard package that includes comprehensive market analysis, property tours, and negotiation, or we can tailor services based on specific needs you may have. This flexibility allows us to work within your budget while still providing valuable support."

Client: "What would a tailored package look like?"

Agent: "For example, if you prefer to handle some of the research or paperwork, we could adjust the fee to reflect that. Alternatively, if you want additional support in areas like negotiating repairs or exploring off-market listings, we can include those services. My goal is for you to feel fully supported, so let's find the right balance for your home search."

Script Five. Explaining Why Transparency is Beneficial

Agent: "One of the recent changes in real estate is increased transparency in agent fees, which allows you to see precisely where your money goes and the value each service brings to your home-buying experience."

Client: "How does that help me as a buyer?"

Agent: "With this transparency, you will have the freedom to understand and choose the level of support you want. I am committed to ensuring you are informed and confident about every aspect of the process, from viewing homes to closing on your new property. Transparency means you have control over the services you receive, and I'm here to make sure those services meet your needs perfectly."

These scripts focus on open communication, personalized service, and explaining the value and benefits of transparent fee structures. They position you as a trusted advisor and help you establish a solid, professional relationship with your clients in the post-settlement landscape.

APPENDIX II. What Is 'FOR SALE'? PART I.

A Sample Buyer Agency Marketing Presentation

This is a marketing presentation framework for a buyer agent to present to potential buyers in the post-NAR settlement environment. This structure emphasizes transparency, value, and adaptability, all of which are essential in building trust and aligning with the new norms.

---

1. Introduction and Context Setting

- **Welcome the Buyer:** Briefly introduce yourself and express appreciation for the opportunity to discuss their home-buying goals.
- **Industry Changes Overview:** Explain how recent shifts in the real estate industry, such as the NAR Settlement, have introduced new levels of transparency and choice for buyers, particularly in how buyer agents work with and represent clients.

- ☐ **Commitment to Transparency**: Emphasize that your approach is centered on transparency, client education, and trust-building to ensure they feel empowered throughout the process.

2. Explaining Your Role and Value as a Buyer Agent

- ☐ **Highlight Key Services**: Outline the specific services you offer, such as market research, property selection, negotiation expertise, contract handling, and closing support.
- ☐ **Tailoring Services to Client Needs**: Emphasize that your approach is flexible, allowing clients to choose the level of service they feel is most valuable.
- ☐ **Demonstrate Expertise**: Briefly mention past success stories or market insights that showcase your knowledge and expertise.

3. Discussing Compensation in a Transparent and Client-Centered Manner

- ☐ **Explain the New Compensation Framework**: Let the buyer know that recent industry changes mean they will have a clearer view of agent compensation and, in some cases, the option to negotiate these fees directly.

- **Break Down the Commission Structure**: Be upfront about how your commission works—whether traditionally paid through the seller's proceeds or an alternative agreement if it suits the buyer's preference.
- **Highlight Value for Investment**: Explain what they receive for this investment, emphasizing your dedication to maximizing their purchase power and ensuring a smooth process.

4. Offering Customization Options

- **Service Packages**: Present options that align with different client needs, from full-service representation to select services based on budget or personal involvement level.
- **Benefits of Each Package**: Clearly outline what is included in each option, reinforcing the flexibility and transparency that allow buyers to choose based on what best serves them.
- **Commitment to Client Satisfaction**: Let the buyer know that your focus is on providing the right balance of services to support their specific home-buying journey.

5. Addressing Questions and Concerns

- ☐ **Open the Floor:** Invite any questions or concerns about the compensation structure, services, or the home-buying process in general.
- ☐ **Reiterate commitment to transparency and value:** Reassure them that your priority is to support them fully, building confidence in the investment they are making in buyer representation.
- ☐ **Provide Additional Resources:** Offer to share educational resources, such as market reports or guides, that help clarify the value of buyer representation in today's market.

6. Closing with a Clear Next Step

- ☐ **Summarize Key Points:** Recap the main benefits of working together—your expertise, transparent approach, flexible service options, and commitment to achieving their goals.
- ☐ **Propose Next Steps:** Offer a specific next step, such as setting up a property tour schedule, signing a buyer-agent agreement, or arranging a follow-up meeting to address any remaining questions.
- ☐ **Express Enthusiasm:** Close with a positive note, expressing your excitement to help them find the

perfect home and your dedication to providing value throughout the entire process.

This framework ensures that your presentation is clear, professional, and client-centered, reinforcing transparency while making it easy for the buyer to understand the value of your representation.

APPENDIX III. What is 'FOR SALE'? PART II.

A Sample Buyer Agency Listing of Offered Fee-Based Realty Services

A Buyer Representation Agreement is a formal contract outlining the general services a buyer agent will provide to a client, along with the terms of compensation, duration, and responsibilities of both parties. In this evolving real estate landscape, agent services may be fee-based, meaning that the standard terms in a Buyer Representation Agreement may not fully convey the specific services offered without an amended and/or appended supplemental scope of services.

A supplemental scope of services enables a buyer agent to present a range of service options and corresponding compensation structures clearly and concisely. This scope of services is a foundation for negotiation between the agent and the prospective buyer client. By incorporating a supplemental scope of services document into your Buyer Representation Agreement, you provide a detailed outline of both the services offered, the services to be performed, and the expected compensation, ensuring transparency and establishing mutual understanding between agent and client. Below is a list of commonly provided services in buyer agency, which can serve as a resource for developing service programs or tailored scopes of service to meet clients' needs at various budget levels.

1. Initial Consultation and Needs Assessment
- ☐ Conduct a preliminary meeting to understand the client's needs, preferences, and budget.
- ☐ Assist with establishing criteria, such as property type, size, location, and amenities.
- ☐ Review the client's financing status and refer them to mortgage professionals if needed.

2. Market Research and Property Search
- ☐ Provide detailed information on neighborhoods, school districts, amenities, and market trends.
- ☐ Use Multiple Listing Services ("MLS") and other resources to identify properties that match the client's criteria.
- ☐ Provide updates on new listings, price changes, and properties scheduled for open houses.

3. Property Tours and Evaluations

- ☐ Schedule and conduct showings of selected properties, either in person or virtually.
- ☐ Offer insights on property features, pros and cons, and alignment with the client's goals.
- ☐ Facilitate access to additional property information, such as seller disclosures or inspection reports.

4. Comparative Market Analysis ("CMA")

- ☐ Prepare a CMA to help the client understand a property's fair market value.
- ☐ Provides data on recent comparable sales, current listings, and local market conditions.
- ☐ Guide the client toward making a competitive offer based on the CMA and market trends.

5. Offer Preparation and Negotiation

- ☐ Draft and present the offer, ensuring compliance with local laws and regulations.
- ☐ Negotiate the terms of the offer, including the purchase price, contingencies, and timelines.
- ☐ Communicate with the listing agent on behalf of the client to reach mutually agreeable terms.

6. Due Diligence and Coordination of Inspections

- ☐ Assist the client in scheduling and coordinating home inspections and any necessary repairs.
- ☐ Review inspection reports with the client, advising on how to address findings.
- ☐ Negotiate inspection-related items with the seller, such as repairs or price adjustments.

7. Contract and Documentation Management

- ☐ Manage all required documents, including purchase agreements, disclosures, and addenda.
- ☐ Ensure compliance with timelines and contingencies outlined in the contract.
- ☐ Assist the client with reviewing, signing, and submitting documents to all relevant parties.

8. Financing and Closing Coordination

- ☐ Work with the client's lender to ensure financing requirements are met before closing.
- ☐ Coordinate with the title company, escrow agent, and other professionals involved in closing.
- ☐ Provide the client with a closing checklist and clarify any final closing costs or fees.

9. Post-Closing Support and Follow-Up

- ☐ Check in with the client after closing to address any questions or concerns.
- ☐ Offer resources, such as local service providers, utility setup, and community information.
- ☐ Stay connected for future real estate needs, providing market updates and property assessments if requested.

10. Compensation and Fee Disclosure

- ☐ Clearly outline the agreed-upon compensation structure, whether commission-based, flat-fee, or hourly.
- ☐ Disclose any seller contributions or adjustments to compensation if the arrangement involves the seller.
- ☐ Confirm the buyer's understanding of the compensation model and ensure transparency regarding all fees.

11. Additional Optional Services

- ☐ **Relocation Assistance:** Provide guidance on school districts, commute times, and neighborhood amenities.
- ☐ **Investment Analysis:** For buyers interested in investment properties, offer rental yield calculations and ROI estimates.

- **Property Management Referrals:** Connect buyers with trusted property management companies if needed.
- **Home Warranty Advice:** Assist buyers in selecting an appropriate home warranty if desired.

This scope of services within a buyer representation agreement clarifies each stage of the agent-client relationship, ensuring a clear understanding of services, responsibilities, and expectations. By outlining these elements, agents establish trust, transparency, and a client-centered approach from the outset.

APPENDIX IV. Implementing the P.I.E.R Approach

Below is a sample of a concise plan to execute the P.I.E.R. Approach (Preparation, Innovation, Engagement & Retention) as a buyer's agent in the post-NAR Settlement environment:

1. Preparation

- ☐ **Market Research**: Stay informed about local market trends, pricing, and inventory levels. Understand neighborhood dynamics and recent sales to set realistic expectations for clients.
- ☐ **Transparency Compliance**: Familiarize yourself with compensation disclosure requirements and prepare to communicate the Buyer Representation Agreement, scope of Realty Services, and fees clearly.
- ☐ **Tailor Service Offerings**: Based on preliminary client information, outline services relevant to their needs and clarify any flexible service options.

2. Innovation

- **Adopt Technology**: Use tools like virtual tours, CRM systems, and data analytics to streamline processes and personalize the client experience.
- **Offer Flexible Service Models**: Provide service packages that align with clients' financial preferences, whether full-service, a la carte, or custom options.
- **Leverage Data**: Provide clients with insights on market conditions and property options based on data analytics, enhancing your advisory role.

3. Engagement
   - **Open Communication**: Maintain regular, proactive updates on new listings, transaction progress, and critical steps in the buying process.
   - **Build Trust**: foster an environment where clients feel comfortable discussing questions or concerns, particularly fees and services.
   - **Personalize interactions**: show understanding of each client's unique needs, including location preferences, budget constraints, and home features, tailoring your approach accordingly.

4. Retention

- **Post-Sale Follow-Up:** Check in with clients after closing to see how they settle in and offer local resources or referrals.
- **Long-Term Engagement:** Provide periodic market updates or home maintenance tips to keep the relationship active.
- **Encourage Feedback:** Seek feedback to improve future services and encourage satisfied clients to share referrals.

By executing the P.I.E.R. Approach with these targeted actions, buyer agents can meet client expectations, foster long-term loyalty, and excel in a transparency-driven market.

APPENDIX V. How to Talk *Compensation.*

Frames for Clear Compensation Discussion Options for Buyer Agents

In the wake of the NAR Settlement, buyer agent compensation has evolved, introducing greater transparency and flexibility into real estate transactions. Here is a breakdown of the fundamental changes:

---

1. Direct Negotiation with Clients

- **Buyer-Paid Commissions:** In the new era, buyer agents may negotiate their fees directly with clients rather than relying solely on seller-paid commissions. This means that agents discuss their compensation upfront with buyers, providing a clearer understanding of what clients are paying for.
- **Transparency in Fee Structures:** Buyers now see a detailed breakdown of agent fees, enabling open discussions and giving them the choice to select services that fit their needs and budget.

2. Flexible Service Packages

- **Customized Service Levels:** Agents can offer various service packages, from basic assistance to full-service representation. Each package can be tailored to reflect different price points, giving buyers control over the level of support they receive.
- **À la carte options:** some agents may introduce à la carte services, where buyers only pay for specific services, like property tours, negotiations, or transaction management, further aligning compensation with client priorities.

3. Seller Contributions in Some Cases

- **Seller-Offered Commissions Still Possible:** In certain markets, sellers may still offer a commission to buyer agents, but it is now more common for these terms to be disclosed upfront, ensuring buyers are aware and can negotiate accordingly.
- **Impact on Purchase Price:** If a seller does contribute to the buyer agent's commission, it may impact the negotiation, allowing buyers to factor in these fees more strategically.

4. Upfront Fee Arrangements or Retainers

- **Alternative Payment Models**: Some agents may adopt retainer fees or upfront payments, especially if they provide extensive consulting or specific services that require early commitment.
- **Adapting to Client Preferences**: This model allows clients to advance payments or pay for specialized support early on, offering more control over how and when they compensate their agent.

In this new landscape, buyer agents are compensated in a way that aligns more closely with the value they bring to the table, making the process more transparent and client-centered. As a buyer agent, this structure enables you to define your worth clearly while clients gain the freedom to choose the services and compensation structures that best meet their needs.

APPENDIX VI. When to Talk *Compensation.*

Key Transaction Frames for Buyer Agent Compensation Discussion and Negotiation

1. **With the Buyer Client: Introducing Compensation During the Buyer Representation Agreement Discussion**
   During the initial presentation of the Buyer Representation Agreement, introduce available Realty Service Plans and associated fee schedules. Following the 2024 NAR Settlement, buyers are responsible for compensating the agent representing their interests. Be transparent and inform prospective clients that agent compensation is a negotiable item. As a diligent buyer's agent, explain that there may be alternative ways to subsidize or transfer the agreed-upon compensation, although these avenues are not guaranteed. These options will be explored further below.

2. **With the Seller Client: Payment of Buyer Agent Compensation by the Seller**

Once a suitable property is found, the buyer's agent should inquire with the listing (seller's) agent to determine if the seller is willing to contribute to or fully cover the buyer's compensation. If the seller agrees to this arrangement, ensure the commitment is documented in writing by completing the necessary cooperative compensation forms. After these forms are fully executed, communicate the outcome of the compensation arrangement to the buyer. Payment to the buyer's agent will follow the documented agreement and will be disbursed at closing.

3. **With the Selling Agent: Payment of Buyer Agent Compensation by the Selling Agent**

    In cases where the seller does not directly compensate the buyer's agent, the listing (selling) agent may offer to split their commission with the buyer's agent. If this occurs, formalize the arrangement by completing and executing the necessary cooperative compensation forms and then communicate the agreed-upon compensation outcome to the buyer. Payment to the buyer's agent will follow the agreed-upon documentation and will be disbursed at closing.

4. **As a Purchase Concession: Buyer Agent Compensation as a Seller Concession**

When neither the seller nor the listing agent agrees to cover the buyer agent's compensation, the buyer's agent may negotiate to have the compensation included as a concession in the purchase agreement. If the seller agrees, ensure the terms are clearly documented in the purchase agreement. Upon acceptance, payment to the buyer's agent will be made according to the documentation and disbursed at closing.

In instances where there is no payment negotiation acceptance by the seller or listing agent, the buyer will be required to compensate the buyer's agent per the terms of the Buyer's compensation agreement.

This framework provides transparency and multiple options for discussing and negotiating buyer agent compensation, aligning with the requirements of the 2024 NAR Settlement, and ensuring clear communication and documentation for all parties involved.

REFERENCES

"NAR Settlement: Get the Facts, NAR Settlement FAQs." National Association of REALTORS®. September 5, 2024. https://www.nar.realtor/the-facts/nar-settlement-faqs.

"The Truth About the NAR Settlement Agreement." National Association of REALTORS®. March 22, 2024. https://www.nar.realtor/magazine/real-estate-news/law-and-ethics/the-truth-about-the-nar-settlement-agreement.

"Welcome to the Residential Real Estate Broker Commissions Antitrust Settlements Website, All Settlements" JND Legal Administration. April 2024. https://www.realestatecommissionlitigation.com.

Christopher Moehrl, Michael Cole, Steve Darnell, Valerie Nager, Jack Ramey, Sawbill Strategic, Inc., Daniel Umpa, and Jane Ruh, on behalf of themselves and all others similarly situated (Plaintiffs) v. The National Association of Realtors ("NAR"), Realogy Holdings Corp., Homeservices of America, Inc., BHH Affiliates, LLC, HSF Affiliates, LLC, The Long & Foster Companies, Inc., Re/Max LLC, and Keller Williams Realty, Inc. Civil

Action No.: 1:19-cv-2544, United States District Court for the Northern District of Illinois, filed June 14, 2019.

Gallagher, Dave. "Attorneys want nearly a quarter billion of NAR, HSoA damages, Using the "one-third" formula, the plaintiffs' lawyers are asking for more than $225 million from the two commissions settlements, plus other expenses." *Real Estate News*. September 16, 2024. https://www.realestatenews.com/2024/09/16/attorneys-want-nearly-a-quarter-billion-of-nar-hsoa-damages.

Han, Brooklyn. "New objection to NAR settlement targets business practice changes, plaintiffs' attorneys fees". HOUSINGWIRE. October 28, 2024. https://www.housingwire.com/articles/new-objection-nar-settlements-business-practice-changes-plaintiffs-attorneys-fees/.

Han, Brooklyn. "Objections Abound as NAR Settlement Approaches Final Approval Date". *HOUSINGWIRE*. October 29, 2024. https://www.housingwire.com/articles/objections-abound-as-nar-settlement-approaches-final-approval-date/.

Regan, Patrick. "NAR settles compensation lawsuits for $418 million and will ban commissions on MLS". *Dallas Agent Magazine*. March 15, 2024.

https://dallasagentmagazine.com/2024/03/15/nar-settles-compensation-lawsuits-for-418-million-and-will-ban-commissions-on-mls/.

Scarcella, Mike. "Realtors' Group Asks US Supreme Court to Block Justice Dept Probe". *Reuters, the news and media division of Thomson Reuters.* October 11, 2024. https://www.reuters.com/legal/government/realtors-group-asks-us-supreme-court-block-justice-dept-probe-2024-10-11/.

Sitzer, Joshua, Amy Winger, Scott Burnett, Rhonda Burnett, Ryan Hendrickson, Jerod Breit, Scott Trupiano, Jeremy Keel, Frances Harvey, Hollee Ellis, and Shelly Dreyer v. RE/MAX Holdings, Inc., Realogy Holdings Corp., National Association of Realtors, Keller Williams Realty, Inc., HomeServices of America, Inc., Re/Max LLC, The Long & Foster Companies, Inc., HSF Affiliates, LLC, and BHH Affiliates, LLC. Case No. 4:2019cv00332, U.S. District Court for the Western District of Missouri, filed April 29, 2019.

Tracey, Melissa Dittman. "NAR Membership Remains Steady Notwithstanding Slower Home Sales". *REALTOR® Magazine.* June 7, 2024. https://www.nar.realtor/magazine/real-estate-news/nar-membership-remains-steady-notwithstanding-slower-home-sales.

United States v. National Association of Real Estate Boards et al. 339 U.S. 485 (1950).

ERICKA L. DAVIS

About the Author

Ericka L. Davis considers herself a "forever student of real estate." Licensed since 2005, she has navigated the highs and lows of the industry, consistently adapting her career to align with market demands. With a passion for sharing her knowledge and strategies, Davis aims to support fellow real estate professionals on their journey. A self-described freelance writer, she holds a Bachelor of Business Administration in Real Estate, an MBA in Supply Chain Management, and an Associate of Applied Science degree in Paralegal Studies, blending academic knowledge with nearly two decades of practical experience as a corporate legal professional, licensed agent and principal broker.

Specializing in buyer brokerage, agent mentorship, and homebuyer education, Davis's diverse background equips her to address the evolving challenges of a dynamic real estate market. By understanding the importance of adaptability in a profession as dynamic as real estate, through her own experiences, Davis has developed a deep appreciation for the value of mentorship and continuous learning. She believes sharing knowledge and fostering collaboration among real estate professionals is key to building a resilient and innovative industry.

Davis's work reflects a commitment to helping others navigate challenges and seize opportunities in their careers. Her debut book, *To Quit or Pivot: Navigating Buyer Agency in the Changing Landscape of Real Estate*, is a testament to her commitment to mentoring agents and empowering them with the tools to adapt, grow, and succeed in an ever-changing industry.

To Quit or Pivot

www.ingramcontent.com/pod-product-compliance
Lightning Source LLC
Chambersburg PA
CBHW051837090426
42736CB00011B/1842